THE ART OF
CO-OPERATION

BENJAMIN CREME

SHARE INTERNATIONAL FOUNDATION
Amsterdam, London, Los Angeles

*The cover picture is reproduced from a painting by Benjamin Creme entitled **Mandala IV** (1964)*

Dedication

This book is dedicated to
my revered Master.
His overshadowing presence
is its inspiration.

CONTENTS

PART THREE
UNITY

PREFACE

The Art of Co-operation is presented, like its predecessor, *The Great Approach — New Light and Life for Humanity*, in three independent but related parts. Each part contains a powerful and enlightening article by my Master followed by a talk or commentary by myself. These provided the keynote talks at conferences in San Francisco, USA; Kerkrade, Holland; and Shiga, Japan. Each is followed by a large section of varied questions arising from the talks.

Part One, 'The Art of Co-operation', which gives its title to the book, discusses at length the opposing ways of approaching and dealing with life: co-operating or competing. It traces the competitive spirit back to the animal kingdom and shows its gradual replacement by co-operation as humanity advances. Many of the problems of the modern world are seen in this context and co-operation is shown as *the* way, in line with our soul's intent, to solve them.

Part Two, 'The Problem of Glamour', tackles the ever-present problem of illusion — glamour is illusion on the astral/emotional plane. It is shown as the fog that hides the truth of reality from most of humanity and causes the pain and suffering of the world. Under the impact of new and powerful energies these glamours are now focused as never before, leading eventually to a great leap forward in human evolution as we free ourselves from their age-old grip.

Part Three, 'Unity', presents the idea of unity from an entirely new standpoint: as the fundamental state which all of us, knowingly or not, are seeking, since it reflects the identity and inter-relation of all atoms in cosmos. Co-operation is seen as an aspect of unity, and essential for its creation. Co-operation and unity are shown as soul qualities, more and more in evidence as humanity grasps the reality of life; and as prerequisites for solving the many problems facing us today. With the teaching and example of Maitreya and His group of Masters to inspire us, we are left in no doubt that we shall overcome these problems and continue joyfully on our journey of evolution.

Background Information

These lectures and answers to questions were addressed primarily to groups familiar with my information and previous publications. Therefore I speak freely about the Lord Maitreya and the Masters of Wisdom, without the need to explain Who They are, Their work and relation to humanity. For new readers, however, some explanation is essential and I offer the following brief account of Their work and plans.

The Masters of Wisdom are a group of perfected men Who have preceded us in evolution and indeed have reached a point where They need no further incarnation on our planet. Nevertheless, They remain on planet Earth to oversee the evolution of the rest of us. They are the custodians of the evolutionary process, the guides, the mentors, the protectors of the race, and work to fulfil the Plan of Evolution of our Planetary Logos through humanity and the lower kingdoms. For many thousands of years They (and Their predecessors) have lived mainly in the remote mountain and desert areas of the world — the Himalaya, Andes, Rockies, Cascades, Carpathians, Atlas, Urals, and the Gobi and other deserts. From these mountain and desert retreats They have overseen and stimulated human evolution from behind the scenes.

For over 500 years They have prepared Themselves for a group return to the everyday world which, I submit, is now in progress. In July 1977, Their head and leader, the Lord Maitreya, Who embodies the Christ Principle (the energy of

Love) and holds the office of World Teacher, descended from His Himalayan retreat and entered London, England, His 'point of focus' in the modern world. Maitreya lives in the Asian community of London as an 'ordinary' man awaiting the appropriate time to come openly before the world. He is expected by religious groups under different names: the Christ; the Imam Mahdi; the Messiah; Krishna; Maitreya Buddha. He does not come as a religious leader but as an educator in the broadest sense.

Maitreya's presence will galvanize humanity into making the necessary changes in our political, economic and social life which will guarantee peace, justice and freedom for all humanity. His major concern is the disparity in living standards between the developed and developing worlds, which, He says, threatens the future of the race. Recent terrorist activity is a symptom of these divisions. Maitreya sees the principle of sharing as the key to the solution of our manifold problems, and the means of bringing humanity into right relationship. Maitreya has said: "Take your brother's need as the measure for your action and solve the problems of the world. There is no other course." Soon Maitreya will be seen on major television in America (unannounced as Maitreya) and His open Mission will begin.

In January 1959 I was contacted by one of the Masters in the Himalayas and soon after by Maitreya, Himself. I was offered the task of preparing the way for Their emergence, creating the climate of hope and expectancy, a task in which I have been engaged now for 28 years. In the course of the training by my Master to prepare me for this work, we have established a moment-to-moment two-way telepathic link. This enables Him to communicate with me with the minimum of His attention and energy. He forged an instrument through whom He could work, and which would be responsive to His slightest impression (of course, with my complete co-operation and without the slightest infringement of my free will). The Master's articles contained in this book were dictated by Him originally for *Share International* magazine.

Further information about Maitreya and the Masters can be found in my books and in *Share International* magazine and website, details of which are given at the end of this book.

I would like to express my gratitude to the many people in London and San Francisco whose time and effort have contributed to this book. Their devotion to the tasks of transcribing, inputting, proof-reading and indexing, cheerfully and efficiently undertaken, have made its publication possible. In particular, I would like to express my gratitude, once again, to Michiko Ishikawa for her invaluable work in organizing the copious material into readable form.

London, June 2002
Benjamin Creme

Editor's Notes:

(1) Throughout the book you will find selected Messages from Maitreya, the World Teacher. During the years of preparation for His emergence, Maitreya gave 140 Messages through Benjamin Creme during public lectures. The Messages inspire readers to spread the news of His reappearance and to work urgently for the rescue of millions suffering from poverty and starvation in a world of plenty. See 'Further Reading' for more information.

(2) Most of the articles, and questions and answers, contained in this book were published originally in *Share International* magazine during the period January 1998 to January 2002. Publication dates are noted at the end of articles and questions. Some questions are from Benjamin Creme's talks in Japan which have not been publshed. They are indicated by 'JC' (Japanese Conference) before the date of each talk.

At the foot of the mountain, My brothers, the climb upward seems steep indeed; but when the first steps have been taken the progress is rapid, and near the mountain top winged feet shall you have, and from that height shall you see the glories of God.

Thus shall it be, My friends and brothers.

I, Maitreya, promise.

From Message No. 89 — 28 November 1979

PART ONE

THE ART OF CO-OPERATION

THE ART OF CO-OPERATION

by the Master —, through Benjamin Creme

More and more, men are beginning to understand the severity of the problems which face them today. On all fronts — political, economic and social — these problems multiply and cause much heartache and sad shaking of heads. Add to these the environmental problems which man's cavalier attitude to nature and its resources has engendered, and the future for mankind looks bleaker still. The realization is dawning that mankind's life is in crisis and that something radical must be done before it is too late.

What, indeed, can man do to save himself from disaster? What steps can he take even to mitigate the threat to his well-being?

The answer is relatively simple but, it would seem, difficult for men to grasp, caught, as they are, in the net of their own conditioning.

Men must release themselves from the poison of competition, must realize it for the glamour which it is, and, seeing the Oneness of all men, embrace co-operation for the General Good. Only co-operation and justice will save men from a disaster of their own making; co-operation and justice alone will guarantee their future. Considering that this is so, man has little option but to accept co-operation as the key to his salvation.

1

When men co-operate rather than compete, they will find a magic potion entering their lives. The ease with which long-lasting problems will be solved will astonish, the impossible will yield to the lightest touch, and, through co-operation alone, men will learn the true art of living. Thus will it be, and thus will men learn to appreciate the beauty of relationship which only co-operation can bestow. Through co-operation the new civilization will be built, the new science revealed, the new understanding manifested. Thus will men grow together in the discovery of their divinity. Thus will they know the joy and happiness of such togetherness.

Central role

The Masters, your Elder Brothers, are not strangers to co-operation. In all that They do, co-operation plays a central role. It could not be otherwise in the manifested Brotherhood where the canker of competition is unknown.

It is Our earnest desire that men learn the art of co-operation, and to this end shall We act as mentors, teaching through example. So liberating is co-operation it is surprising, is it not, that men have been so tardy in learning its joys.

The era of competition is fast coming to an end. With its demise, violence and war, starvation amid plenty, greed and separation, will likewise fade from the memory. To replace these sorrows will emerge blessed co-operation, to guarantee to men their essential divinity. Thus will it be and thus will men come to understand another facet in the nature of God. (*Share International,* September 2000)

CO-OPERATION

by the Master —, through Benjamin Creme

Humanity today stands poised for a great leap into the future, a future in which man's essentially divine nature will demonstrate. Little though he may know this, man has passed and is passing the tests which will allow him, in full adulthood, to become the recipient of knowledge and powers with which to fashion that future.

At present, only to the inner vision of the Guides of the Race may this reality be clear, but such it is, and portends well for the coming time. Wherever men gather, today, can be seen and felt a new urgency, a new sense of commitment to the well-being of the planet and its kingdoms.

Only now, after aeons spent in the struggle for existence and progress, can man be said to have reached maturity, a maturity discernible to Us, albeit well hidden from man himself.

Major advance
The opportunity arises now for a major advance in human progress outstripping by far, in speed and accomplishment, all previous advances. Whereas, until now, a slow and steady progress was desirable, and even preferable, a new, dynamic rhythm is being created whose momentum will sweep humanity into the future on a wave of global change. So great are the tensions in today's divided world that only a rapid change of direction will prevent catastrophe. This rapid change, there is no doubt, will present problems of adjustment to many, but many more, by far, will welcome these changes as the opportunity for new life.

We, the Toilers behind the scenes, have every confidence that humanity will set in motion this radical transformation of its structures. They no longer serve man's needs and block the emergence of the new. We watch and guide, overseeing all.

Little by little, a new consciousness is awakening humanity to its inner needs. The old, competitive spirit dies hard, but nevertheless a new spirit of co-operation is likewise to be seen. This augurs well for the future for it is by co-operation alone that mankind will survive; by co-operation alone that the new civilization will be built; by co-operation only that men can know and demonstrate the inner truth of their divinity.

Co-operation is the natural result of right relationship: right relationship likewise follows wise co-operation. Co-operation holds the key to all successful group effort and is a manifestation of divine goodwill. Without co-operation nothing lasting can be achieved, for co-operation brings into synthesis many diverse points of view.

Co-operation is another word for Unity. Unity and co-operation are the springboards to the future and the guarantee of achievement for all men. Great reservoirs of power lie untapped within humanity waiting for the magic of co-operation to unleash.

Competition strains the natural order; co-operation liberates the goodwill in men. Competition cares only for the self, whereas co-operation works for the highest good of all.

Competition leads to separation, the origin of all sin; co-operation seeks to blend and fuse the many-coloured strands of the one divine life.

Competition has led man to the precipice; co-operation alone will help him find the path.

The old and backward-looking love competition; the new embrace with joy divine co-operation.

The people of the world can be divided into two kinds: those who compete, and those who co-operate.

Cleanse the heart of the stain of competition; open the heart to joyful co-operation. (*Share International*, December 1984)

THE NECESSITY OF CO-OPERATION

[The following article is an edited version of the keynote talk given by Benjamin Creme at the 1997 Transmission Meditation Conference held near San Francisco, USA, and therefore addressed to an American audience.]

The world is divided into two groups: those who are holding on to the old greedy and selfish nationalistic systems and who thus represent the reactionary forces of the world; and those who are opening to the new incoming energies of Aquarius, and who are looking for a way of brotherhood and co-operation, a realization of the interdependence that results from the fact that we are one humanity.

As the one humanity, we are working out our mutual destiny and evolving to give expression — with our different nationalities and talents — to the extraordinary variety of divine life, but in the form of unity. This is obviously a major problem for humanity; the world is so divided, competition is so rife today. It is the very nature of our political and economic systems, based as they are on market forces, commercialization, aggrandizement and power. If we would survive, it must be changed. How can we overturn the tremendous power of competition which underlies all aspects of our life today, and entrench in its place not only the idea but the action of co-operation?

Competition, I believe, is based on fear. If we look back at our history, we can think of competition as it relates to the animal kingdom. It is natural for animals to compete for food in the struggle for survival. There is an ongoing competition between the wolves and the caribou, between the lions and the various branches of antelope and deer. All of these are in competition, but they do not think of it as competition. The lion or tiger never thinks: "I am competing with my brothers and sisters to get at that antelope." It never enters their mind. It is an instinctive reaction to life.

If a lion, tiger or leopard is hungry, it goes out to look for food. Its food is always on four legs, so anything on four legs is fair game to them. It is just a question of who can use its legs faster than the other. If the deer or antelope runs faster, as it very often does, it gets away from the big cat. If, through co-operation, the lions or leopards work together, or, as the wolves do chasing the caribou, co-operate and hunt together by a mutual, inborn instinct of co-operation, they can bring down their quarry, which may be much faster. Co-operation in the animal kingdom works, but hunting is basically a competition for survival.

This is not a historically rigorous account but it serves to illustrate my argument: at one time it was perfectly natural for early man, living sometimes in conditions of food scarcity, to compete for that food to live. They fought for survival. They fought for survival, too, in the ages-long competition between early animal-man and the animal kingdom. The descendants of the dinosaurs — still dinosaurs if smaller and faster, and just as rapacious — decimated humanity. The very existence of humanity was threatened over and over again by the animal kingdom. The instinct of competition for survival is absolutely basic to the animal.

But we are not just animals. Although we owe our bodies and certain of our instincts to the animal kingdom, we are souls in incarnation. As souls, something other than competition comes into play in the relationships between men and men, between groups, between nations. We are not always competing but when we do we always end up destroying ourselves. War is competition writ large, and is something which humanity has turned to again and again for different reasons: for aggrandizement, booty, for pleasure as often as not, as in the Middle Ages, to keep the sword arm strong; for the sheer enjoyment of what replaced the chase — the chase of our brothers and sisters of a different colour, religion, tribe, or race.

With the advent of agrarian civilizations, the necessity for competition diminished. Competition in terms of warfare still took place very often, but the very fact of turning to settled agrarian culture led man away from the necessity of chasing each other, or animals, for the pot. A different aspect evolved: co-operation. Tribes grew in size, little market towns grew up, trading took place. That depends on co-operation. You cannot build a town or a trading station without co-operation. You cannot enlarge the range of human activities and become creative without co-operation. If some are digging the soil, it allows others to build the houses. If some are building the houses, it allows others to play the flute or the harp. These differentiations and specializations enrich human society, civilization and culture. Without the spirit of co-operation none of that richness can be fostered. It needs the sense of oneself as part of a group, a community, brothers and sisters sharing the resources of a particular place, and enjoying, therefore, the fruits of this co-operative interaction.

Overproduction

We have arrived at a point today where, in practical, material terms, the world is probably richer than it has ever been. There are more products per capita in the world than at any time in human history. Never has there been felt the need for so many *things*. Never have there been so many storehouses bulging full with products. We have reached a point of massive overproduction, which takes co-operation to produce but has led to a sustained attack on each other in the competition to sell each other these goods.

At one time people traded for only what they needed. If you produced wine and grew olives, you traded them for gold, silver, tin, lapis lazuli, or some other natural product of the earth. That was sufficient. No one thought of trying to compete with other people in terms of the nature of what was traded. If you were Phoenician, Roman or Greek, you traded with Britain and Germany for the things that Britain and Germany produced, not for what you yourself produced. You gave them wine, olives and marble, and they gave you tin, copper, wool and amber. And so a natural, co-operative, industry of trade grew up in this agrarian culture around the world.

Today, all the nations of the developed world are producing the same things. We all produce motor cars, sewing machines, refrigerators, calculators, computers and all the paraphernalia of our modern, sophisticated city existence — and we are all trying to sell these things to each other. In the main, none of us needs what the other has to sell. We only want it if it costs less. If it is better made and dearer, we do not always want it. If it is better made and cheaper, then we certainly want it. If it is not quite so well made but quite a lot cheaper then we will certainly make do with it. That is how we trade today. We are trading things that we can make perfectly easily ourselves but costing a little more as we do it.

We have reached a kind of impasse in trade. Where is the way from here? One way is to go back to an agrarian culture where everyone makes their own things and trades for what each other needs. That would be sensible, except that the world today is so large, there are so many people, the trading system which would allow that would be so complicated that no one would think of doing it. Of course it would be foolish to try to go back. We have to go in a different direction. We have to become not competitive, but co-operative. Otherwise we shall not go forward in any direction at all.

Competitiveness

Competition, however, seems to be inborn in the human psyche. Everyone, to a greater or lesser extent, is competitive. We have to recognize it, and deal with that fact. Most siblings are competitive: they compete for the love, approval and attention of their parents. If they do not get enough they hate the other sibling and take it out on the younger child. In every family where there are two or three children, the first one is fine until age two when the next one comes along.

The responsibility of parents is enormous. Since competition between siblings is almost inevitable, it has to be controlled and replaced by co-operation which, I believe, has to be taught.

Everyone in today's imperfect society is conditioned. Every parent conditions their children in the way that they were conditioned. We are passing on our conditioning all the time. We have to be very aware, very sensitive and intelligent, to realize what we are doing, and also extremely patient and detached. We have to create the conditions of co-operation for our children from the earliest possible age.

The better nurseries and kindergartens do try to inculcate co-operation. When you see it, it is wonderful, absolutely delightful, but it quickly breaks down as soon as two children want the same toy or the same activity. Then comes the old, primal, primitive man with his instinct to compete, through the desire principle which rules the personality. The astral nature dominates the child until about 14 years of age. (I am not talking about the geniuses who come in as initiates and start painting like Picasso.)

Divine goodwill

The desire principle is very powerful, and instinctively expresses itself through competition. It could co-operate, but grasping, fighting for what it feels it needs, certainly for what it wants, it competes, kills if necessary, hurts, destroys. That is the story of humanity's life until it reaches the stage at which the soul, the divine aspect whose nature is goodwill, demonstrates. As the Master says: *"Co-operation is the demonstration of divine goodwill."* It is the soul which demonstrates goodwill, which makes us want to co-operate.

It is very difficult for human beings in physical bodies, with personalities that are mainly governed by their astral nature, to see clearly, to understand, except perhaps intellectually, the nature of the soul. The soul sees the broad view; it has no sense of itself as separate in any way.

The soul, working magically, produces the person on the physical plane. It creates the ray-structure and the bodies, physical, astral and mental, at a particular rate of vibration determined by the point reached in the previous life. The soul is trying to create an exact replica of itself, and it knows, because it is intelligent, that this will take many incarnations. It has to give its reflection the vehicles which relate to the conditions of life at any given time: the nature of the family and the environment in which it is going to be placed; a set of vehicles, rays and accomplishments. We have had all the rays, more or less, in countless incarnations. Some of them will be in abeyance, not strongly expressing themselves. Others will have been very recently used, and will be clearly showing in the make-up. None of that is ever lost.

The soul has total, absolute goodwill. It knows only divine intelligence, divine love, and divine purpose or will. Goodwill is an aspect of love, the purpose of God and the love of God together, and is essential love. The soul tries to inculcate this in its vehicle, which inevitably leads to co-operation. When you co-operate you express the quality of goodwill. The more co-operative you become the more goodwill you express. The more goodwill you have, the more you will want to co-operate. It is easy to co-operate if you have goodwill. It is difficult to co-operate if you are working under the desire principle, and wanting what your 'intelligence' tells you is needed. The brain intelligence is often at variance with the insight and intuition coming from the soul which always leads to goodwill, to the expression of right relationship.

The soul only knows right relationship. That is what it wants to produce on the physical plane. This of course is difficult since for long ages, and especially now through our modern political and economic structures, we have created a world whose essential nature is competition.

The 'American Dream'

Take, for example, the USA. The greatest desire here, the 'American Dream', is abundance and freedom. Dominated as it is by the 6th ray of idealism, the fundamental nature of the personality expression of America is competition because its idealism and sense of individuality increases its competitive spirit.

The early Pilgrim Fathers came to America for freedom of worship. They found this was a land "flowing with milk and honey". It was the answer to the dream of abundance of material wealth, aggrandizement, power, all that could be said to be worthwhile in the physical life of humanity. That became part of the American Dream. In building this nation the early settlers had to compete for the land which belonged to the Native American tribes; so they had to kill off all the 'Indians', more or less. They brought the gun into play, and, of course, a good gun is better than any good bow-and-arrow. This country was created by competition, as are all pioneering activities. You have to compete to pioneer and build a nation. However, that competitive spirit has lasted until it is the most powerful characteristic of this country.

America's 'gift' to the world as a whole, through its films, the economic and political power which it has taken on itself, is competition. That is the major expression of American life today. It is not the only expression but it is the major one.

From infancy American children are taught to compete. In fact they are made to compete. They are not the only ones, of course. The Europeans, and, above all, the Japanese, are also taught to compete, implored to compete. Mothers only praise their children if they compete well in class. They are taught to welcome every situation which improves their 'chances' in life. That begins to dominate our sense of life, and it has now spread worldwide. It is an American dream which has become a world dream, a dream of abundance.

This dream is based on greed, which is based on fear. It has allied itself with competition which likewise is based on fear. If there is no fear there is no competition. Take away fear and we have the opposite of fear; we have love, confidence, faith. That is removed at our peril. If our parents, in raising us, remove that basic faith in life, that basic trust, love and co-operative spirit of goodwill which we are all born with but which can be fostered or replaced by fear, and therefore competition, competition becomes inbuilt in the consciousness.

Some nations cannot live without competition. Today, a great problem for the world is the American power to influence the mode of living of the rest of the world. It is done, among other things, through radio, television and films. American films are one of the greatest educative tools in the world. They are seen everywhere, in the developed and in the developing world. The US makes good films and bad films but above all films which teach. They teach the world how to live in fear and how to compete to overcome that fear: if you can compete well you can rise above fear. You gain, you aggrandize, you build in plenty, so that you can have a cushion with which to keep at bay the forces of which you are afraid.

This is a country where everyone is taught that the dream of everyone is to 'make a million'. I know that no one in this room has the dream of making a million. You would not be any good at it anyway, because you are too good at understanding the meaning and purpose of life. That is why you are in this kind of group. But millions of people are enthralled with the idea of 'making a million' — the first million, that is the difficult one. As soon as you make one million the rest comes easily. You invest and play the stock market which is built to provide the gaming tables where that million can quickly become two and three million and then a billion. That is part of the American dream.

These people have to live behind locked gates; they have to be passed in and out. You call that freedom? These people never come to my lectures because they finish at 12 o'clock at night and they are afraid they will get mugged. It is the same all over the world. That is not my idea of freedom.

The American people in particular (speaking generally) have accepted this fantasy. They want freedom but create institutions which deny them the very freedom that they are supposed to be wanting and protecting. They build up big armies to protect the American Way of Life. I love America and I love Americans but you can keep 'the American Way of Life'! It has little to do with real freedom; nothing to do with justice or co-operation. It has to do with competition.

Americans are very good at competing, because they do it all the time. They do it in business, they do it in war. And if they cannot do it openly, they do it under the counter, with the CIA. What do you think the CIA is for? The CIA is to compete with the other nations of the world without seeming to do so, because it is not gentlemanly to get rid of democratically elected governments. So you have to bring the CIA in to do the dirty job for you.

I am knocking the United States, but that is not really my intention. I am pointing out the major source of competition, but it has spread throughout the world. And today it threatens the very existence of the world.

Interdependence

If we do not give up competition we will destroy the world. Humanity has to understand that we are interdependent, brothers and sisters of one humanity; also that humanity is a force in the world which has to obey certain rules. These rules are inborn in us from the soul level. When we express ourselves on the soul level we obey the rules.

The rules are that we co-operate. Politically and economically there is no nation in the world, not even the biggest, America, which can stand alone. America has trillions of dollars of national debt, 25 per cent of which is underwritten by Japan. If Japan withdraws its investment in US Government bonds, 25 per cent of your national debt is shaken at its foundation. You have to find the rest or collapse.

This is the result of a complete misconception of the nature of the world on the part of successive governments in this country. The world is different from how successive American administrations have seen it. They have really seen it as a power game, and the bigger, more powerful, you are, the more you can control the game. For centuries the rest of the world has fought out little power games: in Europe for centuries, in the Far East even longer. For thousands of years, China has been torn by strife between the warlords, and the same in Japan.

In the USA, because it is a new country, you have not had that kind of internal strife. That is altogether unusual for a country of this size. You had it twice — the War of

Independence and the Civil War between the North and South. That was your quick (although it did not seem so at the time) telescoping of the history of Europe and the Far East, creating the conditions of modern times. I am sure there are many people in this country who are still suffering from the effects of the Civil War but there are also black people who have been liberated because of the Civil War. There is good and bad in war. There are just wars and totally unjust wars.

What we are waiting for, as the Master Djwhal Khul wrote through Alice Bailey, is the manifestation of the 2nd-ray love of the soul of America. When the soul aspect of America demonstrates, it will rid the world of competition. Until now it has been the personality aspect — which is greedy, presumptuous and aggressive, good at laying down the law, powerfully competitive, and good at that because of its 6th-ray energy — which has largely demonstrated. The 6th ray has a tremendous capacity for galvanizing itself and getting what it wants. The desire principle works through it, and if it did not, of course, it would be a great loss to the world. The last 2,000 years has been a time in which that ray dominated humanity. It is the Piscean inheritance, and it is focused in what is the newest aspect of humanity.

The United States embodies the up-to-the-moment aspect of the Plan of evolution on the planet. America is Europe transferred across the seas — little bits of Europe: Germany, Italy, Britain, Poland, Sweden, and so on. They are taken over and transplanted across the sea and then mixed together. America is the outcome of that experiment carried out by Hierarchy. The people of Europe and America make up the fifth sub-race of the fifth, the Aryan, root race. America exemplifies the latest phase, the latest expression of this development of humanity — from the first sub-race of the first race, up to, now, the fifth sub-race of the fifth race. Out of this fifth sub-race are being drawn now, and over a long period into the future, people who will become the sixth sub-race of the fifth race. They will be found in America and Europe, mainly in America. A new Being is being created out of this mix. Out of the tensions, the possibilities arise for the coming in of the soul factor of intuition.

Achievement

America's soul aspect, the 2nd ray of Love/Wisdom, demonstrated most obviously with the Marshall Plan after the war. The Marshall Plan is the greatest achievement of America to date vis-à-vis the rest of the world. It is not America's gifts of competition, of computerization, getting to the moon, and now looking at Mars. Others do that, more or less. America does it bigger and better because it is bigger and better at those particular things. But these are not the important things — the important thing is the right human relationship which any nation creates. Idealistically, America believes in right human relationships as long as they are along the American notion of what that is. That notion is capitalism and a democratic type of political system — but not too democratic.

Now that the Cold War is over (not through the triumph of capitalism over communism but because Mr Gorbachev, inspired by Maitreya, went to America and talked peace and the ending of the Cold War), there is a degree of co-operation taking place for the first time between America and the former Soviet Union. Russia is likewise dominated by the 6th ray on the personality level. We have had two political, economic and military giants facing and competing with each other, from the Second World War until just a few years ago. There has been a tremendous stress-producing pressure imposed on humanity by these two superpowers. There is now only one superpower, for the time being. (China will emerge as a superpower.) Now that America stands alone as a superpower, it has the responsibility of creating a different world. It will only do so when the 2nd-ray love, the soul aspect of the nation, demonstrates.

Through whom can it demonstrate? Only through the disciples and initiates because they are the ones who give expression to the soul aspect of any nation. It is up to the initiates and disciples to come forward with the ideas, the inspiring thoughtform of co-operation on a global scale, in line with the globalization which America has created in economic terms. There is not yet sufficient goodwill and trust between the nations to create the political counterpart, and so the competitive spirit, in line with market forces, the commercialization of all life which is part of market forces, dominates.

If market forces are to dominate the lifestyle of any global community, then it must be based on competition because the market sets up the competitive base. The biggest will inevitably win. The biggest happens to be America, which is why it fosters market forces ideology. No one is going to foster market forces if they are in an inferior position. You cannot imagine Zaire or Uganda giving to the world the 'gift' of a market-forces economy. It had to come out of this country, the US. Now it has spread throughout the world because your economy has spread throughout the world.

The spiritual crisis of humanity, (not knowing the meaning and purpose of our lives), is focused today through the political, and especially the economic, field, and can only be resolved there. That means that the soul aspect, the spiritual aspect, has to be given expression.

We have to see what we are doing and change it. Humanity has to change or die. This is what my Master spells out so clearly: *"Co-operation is another word for Unity. Unity and co-operation are the springboards to the future and the guarantee of achievement for all men. Great reservoirs of power lie*

17

untapped within humanity waiting for the magic of co-operation to unleash."

Living in conditions of competition and fear, we use only a fragment of our potential. There are billions of people, most of the world's population, who have nothing to say, no part to play in their own destiny. The world passes them by. Life passes them by. They can only look on, abject, exploited, hurt, inwardly furious; angry people watching what happens in the world, seeing it on television and in films. They work perhaps 18 hours a day just to scrape together a poor living. They do the same thing, seven days a week. That is the life of millions of people, and at a somewhat less anguished state, the life of millions more.

What happens when these people see Maitreya, hear His voice calling for justice, sharing and right relationship? These people are waiting for revenge. They have dampened down the fires of their natural lives to not explode, to not kill themselves, to not kill the 'boss'. All of that pent-up, frustrated, life-giving energy is kept from expression now but it will not be for ever. It will take, I believe, everything that Maitreya can do to secure that situation, to keep the pent-up fires within bounds. Maitreya will call for change but, also, you can be sure, for balance and forgiveness. We will see, stage by stage, the growing momentum of change, and will forgive and forget the ancient wrongs. That is an absolute necessity. Otherwise we would have another blood-bath.

Co-operation has to be shown as the *only* way forward, and not simply as an unfortunate necessity: otherwise we would have revolution. We have to *want* the changes for themselves. We have to *want* co-operation. We have to see and accept the rights of every human being, from the youngest and lowest on the economic scale to the princes of power in the mansions of the developed world. That is essential. Competition, as my

Master says, *"strains the natural order; co-operation liberates the goodwill in men"*.

Sub-human existence

If competition is based on fear, which it is, then we are living a sub-human existence all our lives. We accept competition as our job, not seeing it as competition. Our job involves only a part of the mechanism of competition: we must create goods or services cheaper than anyone else. That is the aim. If that means our job goes, that is something we have to accept. Our job goes because we have to 'cut down' to make it possible to sell this particular product cheaper than elsewhere. If you are a good American, and you believe in this myth of competition, you should also accept the loss of your job, your comfort, your way of life. That is a natural part of the market-forces economy.

What if you cannot accept it? What if the strains are too great? The strains of market forces hurt very badly in all of the developed world. It is almost impossible to walk in New York, London, Paris, Tokyo, Berlin and elsewhere without falling over people who are sleeping out — the vast army of homeless and workless of the developed world. This is the creation of market forces. Then there are the drugs, and the crime which arises to pay for the drugs. Eighty-seven per cent of all crime in America is drug-related. It is almost the same in Britain and the rest of Europe. As the crime grows, drugs grow, and as the drug culture grows, crime grows — they interact. Maitreya says that people who suffer from drug abuse are suffering from spiritual starvation. Spiritual starvation, the outcome of competition, drives people to drugs. Of course it makes billions of dollars for the drug barons. They supply the means of slow suicide for millions of people.

How long do we imagine this can go on? We have to change the lifestyle. We have to obliterate from the consciousness of humanity the fear which expresses itself in competition. How do we do it? We have to find a way. We can ask Maitreya, and He will say: "Trust Me, trust life, trust yourself, trust the God within, and share the resources of the world." As soon as we accept the principle of sharing, and create justice in the world thereby, we will come to the end of competition.

The scourge of competition is based on two things: greed and fear. Greed is the outcome of fear. Fear is the basic, fundamental expression of that which is against life. When you take away fear you release the energy of life. This is why the capitalist system is based on freeing people to explore their creativity. However, it is seen in purely individual and materialistic terms; it leaves out the soul aspect which expresses itself collectively. The individuality of which everyone is so proud has to be put *at the service of the group*. When this is done, individuality changes its nature. Instead of being competitive, it becomes co-operative. It expresses divine goodwill. This is what the world has to do. And every group has to do likewise.

Inculcate co-operation in groups

One of the major problems for our groups today, in some countries more than others, is how the groups — who all believe in the same thing, who are all expecting Maitreya, who are putting in time and energy to open the minds of the public to the reappearance of Maitreya and the Masters — contact the media and get them to make this known. All of that depends on co-operation. Right co-operation makes for right outer, and therefore efficient, action, just as focused business efficiency makes for more effective competition.

When you replace competition by co-operation, you bring in the techniques, the awareness, the creativity, the imagination of a bigger group of people. If you work in that way, you are a much more effective group. You get more ideas. You have to see that everyone has a right to their ideas. The ideas are not all of equal merit, perhaps, in relation to the problem, but by co-operation, by trial and error, you arrive at the ideas which are the most effective. This whole question of competition and co-operation is a very relevant group concern which every group should take seriously.

Some individuals just cannot co-operate. To get back to the 6th ray again: the 6th ray, of all the rays, finds it difficult to co-operate because of its marked individuality. The 6th ray is the ray of idealism but the idealism is always individualistically expressed. In every group you will find people, powerfully governed by the 6th ray, who are in such groups because of their idealism. Their motive is totally good, idealistic and worthy, but their mode of procedure, because their idealism is focused in their own individuality, prevents them from co-operating with the other members. They can work *for* the group, sometimes very effectively, but not *with* the group. Co-operation means working with, working together, finding wise compromise. The 6th-ray types find it very difficult to compromise because they are always right. What is the point, they think, of compromising with somebody who is wrong? That is the approach of the 6th ray: it would be stupid to give up my right for their wrong. Only a fool would do that. The 6th-ray person is not a fool. He may be blind, bigoted and obstinate, but that is something else.

Maturity

The Master says that only now — after aeons spent in the struggle for existence through competition — have we come to a point where we can create the necessities of life very easily. We can do it with robots. We will soon do it with super-robots, and eventually will even create the robots by thought. We can do it all, it is not a difficult problem. We have only now reached maturity — a maturity discernible to the Masters, even if well hidden from humanity itself. The Masters know that humanity is mature enough now to think, to measure, to see the possibilities, the dangers, and the ways of action necessary to change.

We have never yet destroyed ourselves. We were on the point of doing it in 1959 during the Berlin crisis, which would have led to the Third World War. That war was stopped, luckily for us, by the mutual action of our Hierarchy and the Space Brothers, through Their representatives in the world. There was another scare in 1962 with the Cuban missile crisis, but curiously enough, that was not so intense. The war against war had been won in 1959, and the earth was saved.

We can still destroy. We have free will; we can reject Maitreya. We can say: "No, we like it the way it is. We are so into competition that we don't know any other way to go." But when the stock markets crash, what then? Is it going to work any more? How can you measure success or failure any more? Huge global corporations are heavily invested in the stock markets, and not only that, they daily, hourly, gamble in the markets worldwide. It is nearly always currency speculation — the future price of the dollar, yen, mark, pound sterling. All the big corporations have a great deal of money involved in that kind of speculation. There are also banks — like Barings Bank (in the UK) — and counties like Orange County (in southern California) which went bankrupt two or three years ago because of their involvement in derivatives, the speculation on the price of any given currency in three or six months or whatever. All of this great edifice, built on competition, can fall overnight, and must be transformed. The Masters know that we are ready, mature enough, to make the right decisions.

The Master says: *"The people of the world can be divided into two kinds: those who compete, and those who co-operate."* That is an extraordinary statement. It seems to me to be the crucial statement about our time, and an extraordinary measure of the state of play in the world, the readiness of the world for change. Two great forces exist today: the reactionaries, looking backward, because they love the past, grimly holding on to the old, the useless, that which is breaking down, falling apart; and those who see that the only way forward is through co-operation, who come into incarnation ready to co-operate because they are disciples and initiates. It is in the hands of these disciples and initiates, who make up the New Group of World Servers, that the future of the world depends. (*Share International*, January/February 1998)

[For information on the ray structures of nations and individuals, see Benjamin Creme, *Maitreya's Mission, Volumes One* and *Two*]

Good evening, My dear friends.
I have taken, again, this opportunity to speak to you, and to
establish firmly in your minds the reasons for My return.

There are many reasons why I should descend and appear once
more among you. Chiefly they are as follows:

My Brothers, the Masters of Wisdom, are scheduled to make Their
group return to the everyday world.
As Their Leader, I, as one of Them, do likewise.
Many there are throughout the world who call Me, beg for My
return. I answer their pleas.
Many more are hungry and perish needlessly, for want of the food
which lies rotting in the storehouses of the world.
Many need My help in other ways: as Teacher, Protector; as Friend
and Guide. It is as all of these I come.

To lead men, if they will accept Me, into the New Time, the New
Country, the glorious future which awaits humanity in this coming
Age; for all of this I come.

I come, too, to show you the Way to God, back to your Source; to
show you that the Way to God is a simple path which all men can
tread; to lead you upwards, into the light of that new Truth
which is the Revelation that I bring. For all of this I come.

Let me take you by the hand and lead you into that beckoning
country, to show you the marvels, the glories of God, which are
yours to behold.

The vanguard of My Masters of Wisdom are now among you.
Soon you will know Them. Help Them in Their work.
Know, too, that They are building the New Age, through you.
Let Them lead and guide, show you the way; and in doing this you
will have served your brothers and sisters well.

Take heart, My friends.
All will be well. All manner of things will be well.

Message No. 2 – 15 September 1977

THE ART OF CO-OPERATION

QUESTIONS AND ANSWERS

[Questions without publication date are from the 1997 conferences in the USA and the Netherlands, and were published in Share International, January/February 1998. Questions marked 'JC' are from Benjamin Creme's 1997 Japanese conference so far unpublished.]

CO-OPERATION FROM THE CRADLE ONWARDS

Co-operation begins as an idea in the mind. Could you talk about the inculcation of co-operation as an attitude of mind?

Co-operation has to start somewhere, and the best place is in infancy. That means the parents must believe in co-operation, must be so soul-oriented that they see co-operation as the better way of living, not only in the family but also beyond the family.

Most families will find, when they take little William or Nancy to kindergarten or nursery school, that their child either fits in or does not. If they fit in, it is usually because they are not overly competitive and have already learned, somewhat, to co-operate. They realize that at sleep or dinner-time you have to be reasonably quiet and not throw too much food around. If you are playing together in the sand or water, you can do it competitively — you can splash and throw sand and have a great time in overcoming your enemy — or you can do it co-operatively and probably get much longer-lasting, if not quite so exciting, fun out of the exercise.

Co-operation is something that the parents have to inculcate. The first child is relatively easy because there is no sibling competition but as soon as the second child comes along there is immediately some competition. The first child will think: "I was the apple of Mummy's and Daddy's eye, and this little brat has come along and stolen my Mummy's and Daddy's affection and time and attention. It is not fair.

Jealousy and competitiveness are based on fear. They are the outcome of a lack of total trust that your mother and father love you just as much as they love the others — and the inability to share that love. Most people find it very difficult to share love. That difficulty comes from childhood. You have to share your mother's and father's love with your siblings and, if that is a problem, it is very difficult as adults to share love with other people. You want the people whom you love to be totally there for you — to show an absolute, total love, fixed on yourself. The fact that they might want to share it with other people is terrible, anathema. Most of us are not sufficiently well brought up, tolerant in that sense, co-operative, to come out of that competitive cycle which the parents set in motion. Competition is everywhere. We see it on television and film. It is in the air we breathe — competitively holding on and making sure that we have all the love and attention, all the things that we desire and think we need.

That is why competition is rife, and stress likewise. People die far earlier than they would normally do because the stress of competition kills the spontaneity of life. Many people just watch the world go by; they are not involved in life, they have no part to play in it. They can only react and never spontaneously create anything except, perhaps, children.

Co-operation, however, is difficult. Parents have to *decide* to bring up their family in co-operation, however they see that. Co-operation is a soul quality: the energy of goodwill expressing itself in a social format.

Inculcating co-operation is the most needed thing but it is up to the parents to do it; that is where it ought to start. Of course, every group should see itself as self-educating, every member of the group being part of a self-educating process. No one has come to the end of the educational phase of their life — it should go on from birth to death — but many people say: "I have gone to school, I am educated," and stop at that. They do not try to educate themselves and expand their consciousness. A huge educational opportunity will present itself to humanity as soon as we take the steps to change the political, and especially the economic, structures. Then co-operation will be seen on all sides because governments, institutions and nations will co-operate. It will then be much easier for individuals to co-operate; it will seem the normal thing to do.

Right Relationship

How can we create an environment, in this very competitive society, in which the new generation can develop their own skills? How do we communicate with them? This question was a result of the generalized thought that the new generations will inspire us to co-operate.

If that is the case, if we are going to rely on the new generations to inspire us to co-operate, you can be sure that the environment has already been set up in which they will show us how to do it. As I have said, children are usually competitive for the love and attention of the parents. I suggested that it is necessary to *teach* children the art of co-operation. I believe that to be true, but I do not think that co-operation on an adult level can be taught. I believe you either compete or co-operate. It is an alternative mode of approach to life; it needs a change of heart.

The fundamental basis of competition is fear. We see, through fear, every person as a potential enemy — someone to

27

put us down, make us afraid, who reminds us of our father or grandfather whom we did not like, who is threatening to us in some way. Where there is total trust, total acceptance of life as we have experienced it, and are experiencing it, competition, and the fear which drives it, does not raise its head. We are either demonstrating who and what we are, or we are not; it is one or the other. If we are constantly demonstrating who and what we are, that is, a soul in incarnation, then inevitably, at whatever point in evolution we may be, that quality of soul will demonstrate.

This is what we see in the infant who as yet has not come up against the competitive spirit in, perhaps, an older sibling. There is a total acceptance and simple moment-to-moment awareness of being in the world. There are beautiful, loving parents ready to give their attention. It is felt as a kind of state of bliss.

Either the soul feeling, sense of Self, is there, or it is not. While it is there competition does not arise. Competition arises when fear comes in — when there is fear of loss, of someone intruding on this total, accepting sense of being at one with all that is. This is an ongoing experience which, from time to time, depending on the point of evolution, is interrupted. It is the state in which that which we call God manifests itself through a human being at the physical-plane level. While the awareness of that connection is held, competition cannot enter because fear is not there. When we talk about competition and co-operation, we are really talking about fear and the absence of fear.

Co-operation is the result of the absence of fear, and has to be introduced to the child. The child has to be shown *by example* how to co-operate — *the demonstration* of the soul quality which we call co-operation, which is the existence of the divine in everyday life. It is that which inspires the child to do likewise. Every child follows its parents, walks behind them, does exactly what they do, talks in the way that the parents talk, approaches life and other people exactly as they do.

When we talk about the responsibility for our child's upbringing in terms of co-operation, we have to know ourselves. We have to demonstrate it ourselves. We have to be who we are — the soul in incarnation. The Master says: *"You can divide the world into two types of people: those who compete and those who co-operate."* It does not mean those who believe in a certain type of competitive economic system and those who do not. That is an effect. It refers to those who in their life are afraid, and those who are not. If you are afraid, inevitably you will compete. That might be in economic terms, but it can be in any human relationship, and so create wrong relationships.

Co-operation is something that has to be *done*. It is an action. It is the result of being who you are, and giving that expression. That will be different for different people because the souls are different; they are individualized, and come in under different ray energies. The quality and manner of that demonstration of co-operation will be different but it will be recognizable for what it is, as right relationship. Every time you say co-operation you have to think equally: "That is right relationship." Create right relationships and you will find you are co-operating. Co-operate and you will find you are creating right relationships. They are synonymous terms.

How can we create a co-operative environment in this very competitive society?

That is the problem. We live in a society in which competition has become like a god. It is accepted as an essential quality of life needed to increase the production and sale of goods. In economic life it has no other function. There is no place for competition, in economic terms, unless it is to produce more goods, more cheaply, and to sell them more cheaply and more consistently than your competitor. What it really means is that we have replaced our sense of ourselves as human beings, as souls in incarnation, with a mechanistic view of the meaning and purpose of life.

It is in *Revelation* in the Bible. The Great Whore has taken over the throne and we worship at this altar of competition and greed. We must recognize this, and nevertheless consistently, at every possible moment, try to produce right human relationships, without sentimentality, naturally, logically, because of who and what we are: a soul in incarnation who, on its own level, already exists in right relationship. The soul only knows the other, the sense of the whole.

We can leave the new generation to itself. Every generation brings into incarnation those equipped with the answers to the problems that they will meet. It is not possible above a certain age to deal with the new situation. The new generation cannot expect their fathers or grandfathers to deal with their problems. The fathers and grandfathers can learn from the young how to solve the problems, and I think that is actually taking place. Many middle-aged and older people may regret much of the activity of the young but recognize also that they have a freedom, a self-confidence, an awareness of the possibilities in life which they themselves only too often did not have or recognize.

Sports

Can sports teach children co-operation, unity and teamwork?

It can teach them teamwork and therefore co-operation. It can teach them unity as a member of a team, and as they identify with the team. It can teach them co-operation because you have to co-operate to play the game.

The best game ever devised for that is cricket because it does not really involve competition — there is no tackling. The competition is symbolic only, between two noble groups — one English and one New Zealand, Australian, West Indian, Pakistani, Indian, Zimbabwean, Sri Lankan or South African. Wherever the Union Jack has travelled, the noble game of cricket has flowered — and cemented there a certain fair and just approach to life, a sensitivity, a refinement of taste and culture. It is an ennobling game. If you can allow your child to join a cricket club, on whatever scale, I would encourage it, because I think there is no greater refining pursuit for the soul in incarnation than the game of cricket. I joke (slightly), of course. Team sports are very good for children. Sports are the sublimation of war. Far better to play games than to play war.

Are people basically competitive and combative?

I think that the civilized veneer on humanity is very thin. We really are, mostly, intelligent animals. Most of humanity are still astrally polarized, controlled by their emotions, so are easily competitive and combative.

'Healthy Competition' — a Rationalization

Is there such a thing as healthy competition in order to make a better, more efficient product or a better medicine?

'Healthy competition' simply brings down the price of a product. If you want cheap products, then you must be willing to put up with the effects of 'healthy competition'. There is no advantage if a product is created cheaply by competition between hundreds of firms, all producing the same thing, if the process involves commercialization, thus diminishing the quality of life.

We need inexpensive products and if, for example, nations did not spend their resources on arms and strategic reserves but instead put the money into producing products at a price people could pay, that could be achieved. You do not need 100 firms all providing the same service and competing 'healthily' among themselves to bring the cost of production down. It might be inexpensive in terms of the dollar tag on it, but what is its cost in social terms? This is the *real* cost.

You cannot cost a product only on a dollar index; you have to look at the social result of producing it. Is it right to squander and misuse the resources needed to build 100 different types of automobiles, drain-pipes, doors, or whatever, in order to get down to the lowest possible price, if the social, global and ecological costs are devastating?

There is no such thing as 'healthy competition'. There is either co-operation or competition. Co-operation is pro-life, pro-evolution; competition is the reverse. It is the opposite of life; it is against evolution. In time, with the use of robots, every nation will become self-sufficient. We will start with the process of sharing by redistributing the resources of the world, which are produced manually or with instruments of various degrees of efficiency.

'Healthy competition' makes an excess of everything, and then the producers compete to sell the product. However, we cannot buy everything that is produced. This is where the myth of choice comes in. Do you buy it because it looks good? Because it lasts a long time? Certainly not for that, not today. Because it is inexpensive? Yes, that is the major consideration. It looks good, and is inexpensive. That is the result of so-called 'healthy competition'.

This process is repeated throughout the world. There are 265 million people in the US. China has 1,200 million people, India 1,000 million, Europe some 350-400 million and Japan 120 million. All of these nations are producing the same goods, more or less — some slightly better, some not quite as good, some more or less expensive. Everyone, however, is misusing the resources of the planet. You cannot have this so-called 'healthy competition' and infinite choice, producing the same goods multiplied 1,000 times, without squandering the resources of the planet. The developed countries cannot buy and use all that they produce. The developing world cannot, for the most part, afford to buy their share at all. Hence the necessity to share.

How do we move away from having many countries producing the same product? Where do we go from here?

It is a question of rationalization. Every nation overproduces something — except some nations of the developing world. Every nation will be asked to make over in trust for the world what they have in excess of their needs; from that common pool the needs of all will be met. The process of redistribution, and the rationalization of our economic structures, will itself rationalize the overproduction process. So we will not have 50 huge firms all producing 'aspirin', for instance, under different names.

This seems so far off.

It will not be done tomorrow but we could do it tomorrow if we wanted to. A country like America could rationalize its production so that it was not creating, through competition, a multiplicity of the same things — and therefore misusing the resources of the world. Go to any big store and you will find the shelves loaded with goods. Where did the goods come from? From the finite resources of the world. Why are they all in this one big store? Why can we buy 50 different types of cleaning liquid, of screwdrivers, or whatever? We do not need that multiplicity.

In the US, because it is based absolutely on the competition of market forces, there is an emphasis on what they call choice. You are given infinite choice — which only wastes your time. The choice is there for this greedy, child-like population that wants, or has been conditioned to want, an infinite variety of products so that one day they want one thing and the next day something else. They feel that this is the great life, that this is 'abundance'. America is about abundance. Every country — Europe, Japan, Australia and the others — have 'bought' this idea of abundance. This is what market forces are about, but the toll in human misery is terrible. In the US alone there are 33 million people living under the poverty line. Hundreds of thousands of people are sleeping in the streets. The social cost of this 'abundance', this multiplicity of choice, is so great that you cannot take it in. Someone should do a study, publish it in a major newspaper, and show what it costs the world for you to have 50 different brands of cornflakes. We can rationalize that tomorrow, and it does not need Maitreya.

Is there anything positive at all within competition that we can use as a way out of competition? Or should we just ignore it and start from the position of right relationship?

If I have been able at all to give my view of the nature of co-operation as against competition, you will see that that is not a real question. Where there is competition there is no co-operation. Where there is co-operation there is no competition. They cannot co-exist. They co-exist in individuals, as that individual changes his or her response to any given situation but they cannot co-exist in themselves. If you are co-operating, automatically competition does not exist. If you are competing, co-operation, right relationship, goodwill, soul expression, unfortunately, go out of the door.

Fear of Loss

Many people of goodwill who have heard our message fear that the ending of competition and the beginning of sharing will mean the loss of their livelihood or status, or even their mode of personal expression in the world. How can we communicate our information to them in less esoteric ways so that they may be less fearful?

Tell them that the principle of sharing does not take away their livelihood; it may well increase it. If you are a multi-millionaire, you are perhaps going to have to put up with a nine-hole rather than an 18-hole golf course in your garden. If you are working as a truck driver, however, you might get a far better life from sharing.

Sharing the world's resources will restore sanity to the world. It will make life happier for *most* people. Some people in the beginning may feel loss through a simplification of life and loss of 'choice' but — under the influence of the Masters, and the spiritual and mental transformation, the loss of tension and stress, which will accrue from sharing — we will create a world in which people will appreciate life even more and find it beautiful. Every day the media will put out information on the progress of sharing and what effect it is having. The entire world will be kept involved. We will see Maitreya on television and He will answer questions. People will say: "You know, I have a bit less money, but I am happier. I am really happy." You can be happier with less when everyone is the same, more or less, when you are not wishing you had a million. Because there *are* those with millions and you have only a pittance. These divisions create greed, the sense of not living life to all the possibilities.

There is no reason why people should think they will suffer from the principle of sharing. Tell them that, on the contrary, most people will live better, happier lives. The people who may not live better will be those who, at the moment, are living at a level which is unreal. You do not need $1 million or more to live a good life. If they make $1 million, and give much of it to charity, that is fine. There is nothing wrong with making $1 million a year if you are giving $800,000 of it to charity — to the developing world, for example.

Karma

In His article the Master says: "Man can be said to have reached maturity, a maturity discernible to Us, albeit well hidden from man himself." Can you elaborate on this? In what sense have we already reached a degree of maturity?

Every disciple, every initiate, is altogether more advanced in terms of spiritual maturity, in the Masters' eyes, than that person is to him or herself. It is difficult for an individual to know precisely his or her state of spiritual Being. A Master does know, and that state can oscillate between one pole and another. It can be intensely radiant at one point and, perhaps, less so at another. This is determined by the service activity and the various karmic difficulties which arise, cyclically, in everyone's life. As you are able to cope with karma, so that karma is loaded on to your back. No one, however, has more karma than they can deal with.

What makes karma a major problem for people is their inability to deal with it, to recognize their own responsibility for it, and to do something about it. Most people blame their problems on other people or on circumstances: it was their upbringing, the fact that their parents did not love them, or got divorced, or left them wanting, or that their husband left them, or did not leave them. All these experiences are shed onto someone else, but of course it is all to do with karma, our own responsibility.

We have to learn to deal with karma equably and say: "That's life; it is, simply, life. *C'est la vie*." Life is another name for karma. What we call 'life' is a flow of karma, good and bad, pleasant or unpleasant — it is all one flow of life. When it is unpleasant we say: "What a life!" When it is pleasant we say: "Isn't life great?" It depends on how we feel, how we respond to the load of karma which we all have to bear. What holds us back in evolution is the karma which is always sitting on our shoulders and is not burnt away in the fire of service. Burn up the karma in the fire of service and you will go like a rocket to the top!

How about humanity as a whole? How is our maturity evidenced?

Our maturity is evidenced by our beginning to take responsibility for our planet on a global scale, albeit in a very tentative, barely discernible way. We are beginning to realize what we are doing to our environment — that we are gradually killing off the planet as a living, breathing, evolving, body of expression of a Great Cosmic Being which, of course, the planet is. We are beginning to see that we cannot go on despoiling the planet, polluting the air, rivers and oceans. More and more, concerned groups have brought this to the attention of governments. At long last, many governments meet on a more or less regular basis to discuss the problems and see what can be done about them.

That is a new maturity, a growing sense by humanity that it is One, brothers and sisters of one humanity, on this planet to carry out some plan, some role, which is as yet dimly felt by most people. That we are, at last, taking seriously what individual groups have for long brought to the notice of governments is a sign that we are recognizing our vulnerability and also our oneness. We are maturing.

For about a century and a half, we have thought it perfectly in order to ravage and despoil the planet for short-term gains — making money, driving industry, all the forces and ideas which brought about the industrial revolution. Now we are faced with the post-industrial revolution, which is a new concept. We are past the age of 19th century industrialization and its refinement in the 20th century, and we do not know what lies ahead. There must be the creation of goods, but most people do not know that it will take a completely different form, using completely different methods which will not despoil the planet. We are now awakening to the urgency of this planetary, ecological problem.

We are even beginning to recognize, on a mass scale — not everywhere but generally speaking — that war is not an answer to our problems. If America wants to go one way and the Soviet Union (as it was) wants to go another, they have to find some compromise, and not just destroy everything in their path to prove a point. Co-operation is beginning to take place. Competition in economics is still there, but in a deeper sense co-operation is raising its beautiful head. The Masters see that, and They nod Their heads with joy. The Masters see that everywhere people are beginning to realize the fundamentals — that co-operation will succeed when nothing else will. We are not yet sharing the resources of the world, but we are talking about it.

Maitreya forecast in the late 1980s that the developed world would cancel the debts of the developing world, as the only way forward. There is no possibility that the developing-world countries can repay the debts. Just recently the British Government decided that this was indeed the mode to be followed. The Chancellor of the Exchequer (the Minister who deals with money and taxes) is starting a worldwide initiative advocating the cancellation of debt. Up until now, the British were one of the most recalcitrant governments relative to the debt problem. America, Britain, and a few others were well behind many governments in advocating cancellation as the only way to deal with the debt of the developing world. Now the British are creating an initiative which, I believe, will end eventually in the fulfilment of Maitreya's prophecy.

Maitreya knows what He is talking about because He already sees it taking place. It could be said for humanity that just as individuals are more mature than they think, the Master sees that the soul itself — the soul in incarnation, that is — is learning, growing and maturing. There is a deeper, esoteric, sense in which the Masters see the new maturity of humanity. They see, for the first time, on a world scale, the correct integration of man's vehicles in relation to the soul. This is a great evolutionary advance.

USA and Competition

Competition seems to be particularly prevalent in the US. Do you think that is indeed the case?

The US is a strange country. Because of the extraordinary power of the 6th-ray idealism of the US, there are communal experiments going on throughout the nation that foster co-operation and goodwill. Comparing the US to any of the European countries, including Britain, there is more community sense, more real desire for co-operation and the expression of goodwill, more manifested love at the goodwill level, in communities in the US. There is, probably, better literature written in the US about creating co-operative communities than anywhere else. But you have to export it. Instead of exporting the concept of competition, you have to export the concept of co-operation. That idealism is the strength of the US.

At the same time you have a terribly competitive spirit, the demonstration of competition as nowhere on earth. Competition is the very nature of political and economic life in the US, and, of course, for that reason is extremely powerful and infectious.

So, too, could be the co-operative spirit, which is being exercised in communities throughout the nation. Co-operative communities are always the result of experiment. They are idealistic, but also pragmatic. People have found that by co-operating they get better communities; they get the facilities denied by your Government.

In the US you have one of those 'hands-off' governments which believes that the government should not intervene — which means *pay for* the services of civic life. I believe that the government should be responsible for the services of the community. In the US you have 'right-wing' governments, even if Democrats are in office. By comparison with a European state they are extremely 'right-wing'. We have the same kind of governments in Europe and elsewhere, but the US 'right-wing' is against spending money on services: it believes all of that should be in private hands, a private industry. It is only a theory and either you believe in the theory or you do not.

We can go on 'till kingdom come' discussing the benefits or otherwise of these different theories. I personally think that the people of any country, *by participatory activity*, should provide for their needs. "We the State" — that is *us*, not the State 'up there', the government, the Prime Minister or the President and his entourage — should provide for the people's needs. I do not separate the state from the people who make it up, provided they have a real degree of participation in the government, in the say-so of how the money is spent.

The entrepreneurial spirit which especially 'right-wing' and which Republican politicians support should be limited, I believe, to more or less the luxury aspects of society. I think that education, healthcare, transport, coal, gas, water, and electrical power (or whatever power we use in the future) should be state-run. They should be national enterprises, run for the benefit of all, and one day, I believe, that is how it will be. The 'embroideries' on that, the cultural and service industries, should be in the hands of entrepreneurial activity. It is the creative action of individuals that can best cater to the refinement of such needs.

After the Second World War the US provided generous assistance to help rebuild a shattered Europe, through the now famous Marshall Plan. Perhaps less well known is the significant amount of money donated by individual citizens in a heartfelt response to the suffering of the European population. Private charities raised $500 million, representing $3 for every man, woman and child in the United States (worth perhaps 20 times as much in today's money). Was this generous response of the American public similar to the outpouring of love that took place recently in Britain following the tragic death of Princess Diana?

Yes. In each case it was the 2nd-ray soul (expressing the Love aspect of Divinity) of the US and Great Britain respectively, which manifested so powerfully. The difference is that the outpouring of love of the British people for Princess Diana was potentized by Maitreya — a kind of rehearsal for the Day of Declaration.

How many initiates are there in the United States who can affect the manifestation of soul energy of the country? (May 1998)

Three thousand, give or take one or two. That is, second-, third-, and fourth-degree initiates. That is not very many but enough for the job. One of them, a fourth-degree initiate, who was Abraham Lincoln, lives in Washington DC. He is a bureaucrat in a minor post in the administration. He will come to the fore, even if unrecognized, and lend his power, insight, and past experience to that group.

Love

Is it the energy of love brought by Maitreya which will truly solve the problem of competition?

Yes, but not alone. Maitreya cannot do it for us. If He could, He would, I am sure. We have to save ourselves, go through the entire process of self-salvation. No one on earth, not even Maitreya, can do it for us. This is a one-to-one dialogue with our soul. We must allow the soul to speak through us, more and more, and call on the soul's energy, insight and awareness by identifying with it. If we never identify with the soul, how can we know it? We have to experience ourselves as a soul in incarnation and, more and more, see that as the reality. When it *is* the reality, the lower man or woman tends to take second place.

The personality will always be there, but it becomes negative in relation to the soul. The soul needs an instrument, a vehicle, a powerful, clear-cut personality through which to demonstrate. It is not a question of negating the personality, putting ourselves down, losing all self-respect. It is a question of becoming more altruistic, more impersonal, more objective.

How can mankind overcome the fear of love? (December 1998)

We can overcome the fear of love by overcoming our fear.

Mankind lives by fear, but when there is no fear, there is love. They are opposites — where you have no love you have fear, and where there is no fear you have love. Love is a natural given state — the nature of the Divinity of this 2nd-ray solar system. When Jesus, acting as the Christ, said: "God is Love," that is what is meant. There are other solar systems whose nature is different — Devotion, Knowledge, or Will or Purpose — but ours is Love. It is our nature, and when we become the soul — that is, when the soul and personality are fused and blended together, which occurs at a certain point in the evolutionary process — we are able to demonstrate the Love nature of the soul. That nature is always there, in every soul. Whatever the ray of the soul, Love is part of its expression in this solar system, because in this system all the rays are sub-rays of the 2nd ray of Love-Wisdom. The great Teachers can be on any of the rays; Jesus is a 6th-ray soul but He showed the Divine Love of God in its perfection by being overshadowed by the Christ, Maitreya, Who is a 2nd-ray soul.

The way, therefore, to demonstrate Love is to overcome fear.

[See Benjamin Creme's article on 'The overcoming of fear' in *Maitreya's Mission, Volume Two*, Chapter 10.]

The problems of mankind are real but solvable.
The solution lies within your grasp.

Take your brother's need as the measure for your action
and solve the problems of the world.

There is no other course.

From Message No. 52 – 28 November 1978

CO-OPERATION AND GROUP WORK

What does it mean truly to co-operate as a group?

It means not to be destructive. It means to do things with a common sense of purpose, with a consensus of opinion on direction and policy.

Is the energy of competition really a problem in group work?

I think it is one of the major problems. People compete for 'success' within a group. They compete for prestige or status. In London, from the very beginning, we have had no officers. No one has a title, so there is no kind of status in that sense. There is status in the sense of effectiveness. Some people work harder, more assiduously, and more efficiently in making the information known, or just in the general office work that goes into putting out the information. Whether selling cornflakes or making known the Reappearance, you still have to package it in some way, and that is office work. Some people are very good at office work but they get very little kudos out of it.

Other people might make approaches to the media, and think they will get more kudos. Everyone wants to talk to the media, except 2nd-ray types. They want to but are afraid. In almost every group I have ever known there are people who say: "I would love to talk to the media, leave it to me." They are always the worst possible people to do it. They have no idea what they should say, little idea of what we really are about, no knowledge of how every word given to the media will be twisted and distorted. The people who really can talk to the journalists tend not to realize it, perhaps, and do not come forward.

Competition in group work is, perhaps, not always voiced, but it is there and you have to recognize it. Every group has its problems, and competition voiced, or not voiced, subtle or otherwise, is destructive in a group.

We know intellectually that we should not compete, but a competitiveness creeps in subtly. What can we do?

Who said it was subtle? It just storms in! I know individuals, every group has them, who cannot do anything from other than a competitive spirit. Three-quarters of the year they do nothing, but then they suddenly get a little bit inspired. They do a little bit: they approach the media and everyone has to hear about it. We have to know everything that a certain individual does. We have to know how hard they are trying, how well they are doing, how much the group depends on their visit to a bookshop. Everyone has to know that a certain bookshop *might* take some books. It is already an achievement!

It is competition with the other people in the group. It is not only deadly boring, it is very destructive, because people make their alignments, and cliques develop. As like attracts like, those who are competitive attract each other. Those who are co-operative are repulsed by that competition. And so the group loses its coherence. That is why it is absolutely essential that the competitive spirit be replaced.

Does an understanding of the wider mission of the group help in the process of co-operation?

If you are idealistic, it should. If you are competitive, if you do not see the wider implications of the group, then you might end up being very destructive. Perhaps you should be put out of the group if you are very competitive and destructive. It is up to the group itself. The wider mission of the group should tend to make you think twice before being destructive. It should help you to look at yourself with greater insight and to bring a more co-operative attitude to bear, even with people with whom you are normally competitive, and do not like.

How much patience must we show towards people who will not respect what is being done within the group? Sometimes you have to draw a line.

As much as is necessary. You have to assess how much that is because every problem and situation is different. I know there are impossible people in every group. The impossibles you have to live with, or put out, one or the other, leaving the others to enjoy the group work. Group work should be enjoyment. Someone mentioned the joy that can come out of a satisfactory, full-blooded group activity. It is true. Group work should be the most joyful work that exists, far better than working alone, although personally I love working alone — that is, as a painter.

Are group working sessions useful to clarify individuals' points of view and try to achieve a common group goal?

If you like group work sessions, by all means do it. You have to try, see what works. Some people like bringing up different points of view in a group situation, mulling over and putting forward the different points. Many people get a lot out of that, so why not do it?

Noting that the title of the Master's article is "Co" hyphen "operation", we observed that this group appears to have realized the "Co-" part as in co-operatively recognizing its task, and in non-competitively trying to accomplish it, but that we tend to fail in the "operation" part, putting theory into practice. How can the groups around the world better co-operate in total to accomplish their task?

If you find it difficult to co-operate effectively in your own group how can you possibly expect to co-operate with the other groups worldwide?

Actually, that world co-operation is already taking place: the production of *Share International*, together with *The Emergence Quarterly* and my books in translation, and the fact that some of us are in constant contact with these various groups, demonstrates and ensures that global co-operation in this work is a reality.

The Masters are trying to demonstrate something as a group, so we should remember that it is bound to be difficult for us.

They are quite good at it, actually. Demonstrate the Love aspect of God, that They *can* do; They really know how it is done; They have been doing it for a long time. Even the most recently-made Master is a Master because He *can* do it. It comes naturally to Them to demonstrate total, unconditional love. It comes naturally to have the wisdom of all the ages at Their fingertips, because that is the nature of the expanded, illumined mind of the Master. They really are good at it. It is bound to be difficult for us, because we are only half animal, half man!

Motive

It is imperative to be watchful of one's own motives and the tendency to compare and compete, isn't it?

Absolutely. Comparing, of course, is the essence of competition. You compare yourself and your little achievement with others who are doing a lot of work. If they are rather good-looking and energetic, you say: "I hate that person, thinking she's the top." In every group there is someone like this, who comes in and does work that makes the old hands feel inadequate, because he/she is effective, and does not have the old hang-ups. Maybe they are younger, and have had less time in the work so they are not so blasé. They have not lost the impetus and enthusiasm and so they make the others feel inadequate. Then jealousy comes in and, with that, the competition. It is the same with children. The elder brother and sister are competing with the younger one. The younger one is jealous of the older one. It is in the nature of the sibling situation, and a group becomes rather like a family, so the same situation pertains.

As the questioner says, we must look at our motives. You have to be pure in your actions, which is not easy. You have to be pure, too, in the sense of really looking at your motives, even if you cannot change your actions. If you continually look at your motives, and assess the true, underlying intention behind everything you say and do, you gradually become pure. You act spontaneously in the right way. You are not competitive.

You have to learn when not to say anything at all. I have found in many groups that there are those who protect the group. They would like to be more open, more powerful, more efficient, but they do not want to do so because it always arouses jealousy and competition from the others. They have to keep themselves somewhat *sotto voce*, hold themselves in, not say too much because they will be branded as a 'big-head' or 'loud-mouth'. These are the dynamics in every group, and have to be faced, because the people involved are ordinary people. They are also disciples of some degree, and so the whole aspect of motive has to be carefully looked at.

No one is totally pure. I meet people in every group who, when they speak to me, are not speaking to me straight. They are saying what they think I would like to hear, or what they would like me to believe. It is better that people say simply what they have to say. There is a time for criticism of a constructive nature, but there is no time for destructive criticism coming

49

from jealousy, fear, hatred or maliciousness. We have to watch our motives in all these situations. This is a must, fundamental. Until we really are speaking from the centre of ourselves, acting as a group from the centre of ourselves, without these motives of competition, jealousy, fear and sullen resentment, we will never achieve correct co-operation. That destroys the goodwill which is at the basis of co-operation.

It is difficult to watch myself. How is it to be done? (JC May 1997)

The difficulty of watching oneself is to do with glamour. It is precisely glamour that prevents the mind from being sufficiently objective to look at and recognize the action of the other vehicles and itself. The beauty of the evolutionary process is that gradually you overcome glamour. You overcome this illusion, this fog, in which 99 per cent of people live. Up until the first initiation, the individual is completely surrounded by glamour. The period between 1.1 or 1.2 up to about 1.4 to 1.5 is a period of intense glamour and the pain of that glamour. Up until 1.2 or 1.3, the person does not even see the glamour. He or she is so lost in it; for them the glamour is the reality. As the person evolves, the soul, through the mind, throws a light on the glamour. The person then becomes aware of the glamour, but cannot do too much about it.

The gradual process towards mental polarization, as distinct from astral polarization, frees the individual from the fog of that glamour. At about 1.5 to 1.6 the shift is made between astral polarization and mental polarization. Mental polarization is not complete at this point. It is not complete until 2.5, but from 1.5 to 1.6 and up to the second initiation, there is a growing capacity to see quite clearly the difference between glamour and reality. This is the beauty of Transmission Meditation. It speeds up the process whereby you can shift from astral to mental and eventually to spiritual polarization. The most difficult period is between about 1.3 to 1.6. It is not easy.

[For information on Transmission Meditation, see Benjamin Creme, *Transmission — A Meditation for the New Age*]

It is easier to see others. It is more difficult to watch myself. Is this because of glamour? (JC May 1997)

We imagine it is easier to see others. It is easy to think we see others, but we are often only projecting onto others what we think they are. That is a major glamour. We do not really see others.

My understanding is that we can only see others at the level of where our self-awareness has reached. Is that correct? (JC May 1997)

Yes. It was previously said: "We can see others, but we cannot see ourselves." I say, no, you imagine you see others, and there comes a stage of clarity in which you do objectively see others, but that is really a rather advanced stage. Until that point, we are simply projecting our mental prejudices onto others, usually disliking in them our strongest bad points.

When we recognize a competitive edge in ourselves, we tend to put ourselves down, or suppress it, but it is still there. We focus on the work, on the goal, but our conditioning is very strong. How do we "cleanse the heart of the stain of competition"? Shift from astral to mental? Mantras? Soul light? Transmission Meditation?

All of these. The best way is to rise from astral to mental polarization, and as that is achieved, as soon as possible, from mental to spiritual polarization, because the higher you are polarized the more the soul can influence the personality life. It is the soul which is co-operative. The soul does not know what competition is. It knows only goodwill, and it is through goodwill that co-operation comes. If goodwill is not there, you can talk about co-operation, you can try, intellectually, all your life but it will not be there, because goodwill is fundamental.

The first thing that everyone has to have in a group is goodwill towards each other. Goodwill is the cement that holds the group together. The more you can see people in terms of the soul, rather than in terms of the edgy, difficult, unlikable personality, the more you will be able to act co-operatively without resentment.

Is the energy of goodwill the lubrication for group work?

The energy of goodwill is not only the lubrication of group work, it is the very basis of the existence of the group. This is what people perhaps do not understand. There are *only* groups. We talk about group initiation as an unusual thing, but actually initiation has always been a group activity, only we have not seen the groups. The difference is that now, under the incoming energy of Aquarius, people are forming themselves into groups. So the idea of group initiation can become a real image in people's minds. Actually there has never been anything else but group initiation. But it has always been a man here, a woman there, slowly, in an individual way. Now the same numbers of people, in group relationship, will take initiation. It is a different mechanism because the inner groups are being replicated on the outer physical plane. They still remain the same groups on the inner plane — groups to which all these individual people belong. The difference is that it becomes a conscious group activity.

[For more details on group initiation, see Benjamin Creme, *Maitreya's Mission, Volume Two*, Chapter 19]

Opportunity for Service

How difficult is it to achieve this kind of co-operation in a group sense?

It is difficult, because of our conditioning and our point in evolution. Change is slow, and we have to accept that. However, we are working in groups, and in conditions of experimentation. We have to take that as the basic reality and seek to put into our work what we know.

We are very lucky as a group. We are not working vaguely for self-advancement or self-development — at least I hope we are not. I hope no one here is simply in these groups for possible self-advancement or self-development. We are here to serve the Plan of Evolution in so far as we have been presented with an aspect of that Plan — not only an aspect but one of the *major* aspects of that Plan: preparation for the externalization of the Spiritual Hierarchy on to the outer plane. That is momentous.

We are living in momentous times; I cannot say it strongly enough. This is a time unlike any there has ever been before. I doubt if this particular opportunity for service has ever been presented to a group before. Many times in His Messages Maitreya has said: *"This is an opportunity for service unlike ought seen before."* If He says it, you can be sure it is a reality. Never have so many people had this opportunity for service, this opportunity — at their level — to do something of *major* importance. That is why groups like this should recognize the opportunity, and the privilege given by it, to do their very best to live up to the opportunity presented and not waste it in competition or greed, or simple self-awareness and self-contemplation — which everyone has moments of but which, with dedication to the work, should be very rarely seen.

How does one set priorities in one's involvement with the group work? I have trouble keeping a balance. (JC May 1997)

It is important to reach a balance between the inner and the outer. Transmission Meditation is not simply to do with the inner life. It is an act of service on the physical plane. It is part of the outer service activity as well as an inner experience. Every individual has different requirements, different amounts of energy, different aspirations, different demands on his or her time, depending on their job and their leisure time. You have to make certain decisions and, therefore, certain compromises in your life. The choices for a disciple are the choices between priorities. They are all priorities, but you have to make choices between the priorities.

Most people have to earn a living. That is the number one priority, which means they will have, to some degree, limited time for service. The priority for the disciple therefore, will be how to maximize the value of that time. It will depend to some extent on your rays, your aptitudes, your involvement with either Transmission Meditation and/or outreach activities as to which of these activities you give the major proportion of your time and energy. Every individual's possibilities are different, so every individual has to make that decision, that alignment of priorities for him or herself. I cannot say you should give 70 per cent of your time to Transmission Meditation and 30 per cent to other work, or vice versa. It depends on the individual, the nature of their work and the importance of the work. It is all important. I would advocate for serious disciples, group members, three hours of Transmission Meditation three times a week, nine hours a week. That means, if you have a job, you have four other days in the week in which to carry out other aspects of your service activity, whether that is producing *Share International*, outreach to the public, or organizing lectures and fairs. If you are prepared to have no social life, no family life, no other life but one of service, that is the ideal, but it is up to you. The Masters are not tyrants, but since They work every second, 24 hours a day without sleep or food, without cessation, it means They have a rather high standard of service to judge by.

Detachment

How can detachment be utilized to deal with the effects of competition within the group?

Become more detached. Ask yourself: "Who is competitive?", not "Am I competitive?" Of course you are competitive; everybody is. Find out *who* is. If you distance yourself from the competitiveness and identify with the "who", then you become more detached. The more detached you become the easier it is to be detached; it becomes a habit. The thing is to look at *what is happening*, and to detach from that by not identifying.

Ask yourself: "Who is competitive? Who is hurting? Who is upsetting the group? Who is destructive?" Find out who it is, which of the demons, because it is one of your demons. We all have lots of demons. But if you just say: "I mustn't be, I must try not to be," you do not do anything. The demons have many heads, and every time you cut off one head another one takes its place. The more effort you put into not being competitive, the more competitive you will become. You have to *replace* it with something — co-operation. That comes from the soul, from meditation, through right identification.

Do we learn to co-operate by developing detachment, sincerity of spirit, honesty of mind, awareness, unconditional love, etc, or do we learn these skills by co-operation, by being co-operative?

It is really a question of both. If you are detached, it is easy. But how many people are detached? You can develop detachment, and as soon as you act from detachment you are already co-operating, you are already in right relationship. It is not something you have to learn. Detachment, sincerity of spirit, honesty of mind, awareness, are themselves the result of a co-operative attitude, and, demonstrated, lead to co-operation. You cannot separate these things: right relationship is another word for co-operation, which is another word, as the Master put it, for unity. Unity, co-operation and right relationship are three different ways of expressing the same thing.

Does Transmission Meditation bring co-operation within a group?

Anything that brings you into contact with the soul, and energizes the vehicles of the soul, will tend to work in that direction. I cannot say: "Do Transmission Meditation and you will learn to co-operate." It is not as simple as that. Co-operation will become more and more part of your nature if you do Transmission Meditation correctly, assiduously, with your attention in the head. It will bring about the reorientation which is needed.

How to Inculcate the Co-operative Attitude

You said: "Co-operation is an attitude of mind and an experience of one's own way of looking at the meaning of life." Is there any practice we should be conscious of in our group work in order to inculcate such an attitude? (JC May 1997)

One of the big things is to be open to other people's ideas. Listening to other people's ideas and allowing the time factor to open the way for the generation of other ideas is creative thinking. The problem is that there is an absence of this in the world.

We say: "Maitreya Buddha, the Christ, is in the world." The Buddhists would say: "Not possible. There are another 5,670 million years yet to go before He can come." The media would say: "Not possible. Whoever heard of such a ridiculous idea?" They immediately close to any such possibility. We might object to this and say: "It is not fair. How can we get the message out?" But most of us do the same sort of thing in our groups.

Those who are used to making decisions and announcing activities tend to believe they know everything. Then at a meeting there is some quiet person, who does not speak very much, who does not have many brilliant ideas, who suddenly speaks up and mentions something. Usually the bossy one will immediately put them down. "No, we are not doing that. We are doing this. I have decided." A more creative approach would be to think laterally about that. "Well, let us listen. On the face of it, it does not sound too promising, but let us think around it." In thinking around it perhaps something emerges which was not apparent in the idea or the presentation of the idea, but which comes out when a discussion is held. This attitude requires a basic respect of every individual in the group.

There should be a renewed practice, not study, of the attitude of mind which we call co-operation and flexibility. A study of Maitreya's teachings, in a very definite way, is an enhancement of the sense of being, the evolution of one's being. If you practice honesty of mind, sincerity of spirit, and detachment as the way towards Self-awareness and eventual Self-realization, and at the same time present to the world the teachings of justice, sharing, co-operation, right relationship, and peace, you become more convincing. Nothing convinces others like seeing these attitudes in action. By the same token, nothing is more unconvincing than seeing people who present information about the Reappearance, about the need for justice, sharing and peace who in their private life and their group work act with domineering, manipulating guile and have none of the qualities that they are talking about.

Practice the qualities you are talking about. Otherwise, there is no honesty of mind, or sincerity of spirit, and therefore, no detachment. Practice these three to your heart's content together with co-operation, which is already changing the groups, and add flexibility to that. Then there will be nothing that can stop you.

Do we promote co-operative activity in our group by striving towards mental polarization?

You cannot strive towards mental polarization. You can become mentally polarized but striving is not the way to do it. One way is to put more time into Transmission Meditation. It is not so much more time as a higher focus, keeping the attention at the ajna centre for more than the three-and-a-half minutes per hour that, probably, you are doing.

Do we promote co-operative activity by not under-estimating ourselves and our abilities?

I quite agree. It is true that you should not under-estimate yourself, because you never know what you know until you start to speak, and you never know what you can do until you actually get to work and do it.

Everyone thinks of themselves as they are now, but everyone is the sum total of hundreds of thousands of incarnations — think of the number of times you have had all the different rays, the number of experiences everyone in this room has had. All of that is there. You have only to tune in to it, bring it out, try it. It comes back, and you will find you can do things that you never knew you could do.

Co-operation and Flexibility

When there is a task to do, it is easy to get people to co-operate in performing the task. The difficulty is in carrying out the day-to-day, ongoing activities. (JC May 1997)

Of course, if you have certain clear-cut, defined tasks, and you ask people to work together to perform them, a group of this kind would, nine times out of 10, be able to work in that way, especially keeping in mind the idea of co-operation. Many groups here in Japan have succeeded far better than at any time in the past in working in that co-operative way.

If a group is not functioning in a co-operative manner, you have to look at the inner dynamics of the group. This can be a changing situation as people join or leave groups. But for a given period of time the group will be able to co-operate, or be based on personality competition. Those groups which have not succeeded to any extent in furthering their ability to co-operate over the last year, are precisely those in which personality competition is and always has been rife. The basic components of the group are setting up a dynamic of competition. That is against group work, against group evolution.

This is where the other aspect, flexibility, overlaps into co-operation. Why did I mention the need to inculcate flexibility this time last year? Simply because I was talking to the Japanese groups. In Japan it is necessary to talk about the need for flexibility because it is a very old, tradition-bound country in which flexibility is not present to any great degree. It is out of the ray of personality (7th ray) of the past. It makes for a very static and rigid society that is only now breaking out of that mould.

The question of personal glamours also enters in. There are people who believe they are co-operating when, in fact, they do nothing at all in that way and are totally inflexible and competitive with other members of the group, whether consciously or unconsciously. The very essence of glamour is that it is unconscious. If you see the glamour, you have the chance of getting out of it. If you are unconscious, if you do not even see it, then you do not recognize it as glamour. I do not want to set up a competition between the different groups to see who is making the most evolution, who is really co-operating and who is not. It is a fact, however, that some groups are evolving quickly, in a group sense, through co-operation. They attempt to deal with inflexibility. There are other groups and individuals who are still lost in the glamour of competition, not recognizing it for what it is. Therefore, these particular groups are not making the evolution that the others are making.

[For more information on the rays and nations, see Benjamin Creme, *Maitreya's Mission, Volumes One, Two, Three*]

How can we discriminate between flexible work methods and manipulative ones? (January/February 2000)

Dispassionate, objective working in a flexible manner will aid the work of the group, and that will be obvious; there will be, of course, a method agreed to by the group as a whole. Manipulative work is the attempt of individuals to impose a method or structure on other people. It is an infringement of free will, and it should be obvious whether there is an agreed group method or a method imposed on the group by one or more people.

Flexible work will actually be flexible, able to respond to the need as it presents itself. Manipulative work can be flexible or rigid. It has nothing to do with flexibility. It is the intent to get other people to do what you want them to do. You can manipulate the situation in such a way that you impose rigidity, not flexibility, on the actions of the group. It is a question of the approach. If the question were posed: "Is a flexible approach to work valuable?", I would say: "Yes, very much so." "Is a manipulative approach to any situation, work or otherwise, valuable?" I would say: "No, absolutely not."

If, in arriving at compromise within a group, there is too great a suppression of one's own thoughts and ideas, is this really practising honesty of mind? Where does one draw the line between honesty of mind and the ability to compromise? (JC May 1997)

Honesty of mind does not consist of holding on to your opinion whether it has been proved right or not. Honesty of mind is thinking and acting in a straight line between your thought and your action. It does not mean you should not put your own ideas aside in order to reach a compromise with people who are at the opposite end of the spectrum to yourself. If that were the case, compromise would be impossible. Therefore, all evolution, even peace itself, would forever be impossible.

If the Prime Minister of Israel cannot compromise, cannot see the rights of the Palestinian people and seek a wise compromise between the different aspirations and sense of requirements, there will never be peace in the Middle East. If there is no peace in the Middle East, there will never be peace in the world. So it is absolutely essential that they learn to compromise.

The rays of most groups, sooner or later, can bring them to compromise. Most groups are able to compromise in the end, even if not immediately. There is one ray, the 6th ray, which finds it difficult to compromise. It is the "nature of the beast" as we say. The problem with Japan and Russia concerning that little group of uninhabited islands north of Japan has been an inability to compromise. Neither wants the islands themselves, but they want control of them. There might be oil there. Or if the

Russians hold onto them, they might want to put a garrison there, perhaps one man on each island to frighten the Japanese! The people of Northern Ireland share the same rays — the 6th ray, through and through, major and minor ray. It has taken years to bring them to the conference table to discuss their problems.

Wherever there are people who cannot co-operate, there are always dominant 6th-ray characteristics. That presents the problem of co-operation, because they cannot compromise. Their way is the *only* possible way — it is all they can see. Of course, this is not true, but for them it is true. There is no individual in any of the groups who has the monopoly of wisdom, intelligence and articulateness.

A group is a group because it requires all the qualities which a group has in order to do the work properly. The art of group work is to focus these different points of view, attitudes, talents and experience into a tool which can speak for the whole group through consensus. There are people who imagine that their ideas are better than all the other ideas put together. They are probably totally unconscious of this and would deny it if it were put to them. Fundamentally they are in competition with other members of the group. There should be the constant intent to put the qualities of co-operation and flexibility into every aspect of your group relationship.

You have to look at your motive at every moment. You have to free yourself from this constant competition, because it is ingrained in every person in the world today. Then, without thinking about it, spontaneously, you become co-operative. Whatever you do is co-operative. If you rid yourself of competition, you cannot help but be co-operative.

What does co-operation and democracy mean in terms of group work? (JC May 1997)

Co-operation means the attitude of co-operation. It means there is co-operation between individuals in a group. Otherwise, it is not a group. It also means co-operation between one group and another. A group is made up of individuals, some of them more dominant than others. These groups can, and if it is a positive thing, should, influence each other. That is the value of co-operation. My own preference would be to have the maximum degree of democracy in all the groups. However, I know the idea of democracy is only a very recent experience for the Japanese in the political field, and therefore, in the way of working together. Some groups are more democratic than others in their management and group relationships. If that kind of influence can grow, I would see it as a good thing. The groups that are more autocratic, more individualized, that are more under the direction of one or two individuals, are to my mind of less long-term value to the Japanese people than those which are functioning truly in a democratic fashion.

This is where flexibility comes in. It is necessary for the more autocratic or traditional-minded groups to become more flexible and move towards a more democratic way of working. Those groups who are already working this way can usefully influence the others by showing that it works. It depends to some extent upon where the groups are situated. Usually, the more urban areas, the key cities, tend to bring in newer and fresher ideas before country districts. But in Japan, nothing is clear-cut. Everything is going in different directions at the same time. It is to some degree a question of what works rather than setting up an ideal and breaking your backs trying to fulfil the ideal. Get on with what works. Time is also a factor.

Free Will

When there is a task that someone must do and group members recognize it, some say it is their free will to refuse. I think they should co-operate and do it, even if it seems a little bit difficult. Can we make them do it, or should we respect their free will and leave them alone? (JC May 1997)

How do you make someone do a task if they do not want to do it? Do you point a gun or stop their beer allowance?

If there were a task that someone must do and group members recognize it, in any self-respecting group working as a group, there would be a 'free-for-all' to see who could get there first and do the task. If no one will do the job, whatever it is, and someone is smaller than the others, the others might feel that they can force him to do it, but to my mind this is not on. The infringement of free will is never allowed. Maitreya has close to Him people who have been invited to appear on television, to talk about the World Teacher, and they refused to do it. Maitreya does not use any effort at all, not even persuasion. He just says: "Well, somebody has to do it." These are people who see Him every day, more or less. His presence would become known much more quickly, at least in Britain, if they would come on television and talk about it. So it is left to me to try to get the media to pay attention. Free will is sacred. Service has to be done from free will, otherwise it is not service.

Concerning free will, a senior member of a group sometimes asks a newcomer: "Can you do this or that?" This seems to me an infringement of free will, yet I think this will give the newcomer an opportunity to participate in the group work. What do you think about this? What is leadership in group work? How should the leader make his leadership effective in the group work? (JC May 1997)

Where there is this emphasis on leadership, it is the opposite of group work. The concept of a group around a leader who guides them and teaches them and leads them forward is an old Piscean concept. It is disappearing fast, or should be. In groups connected with the new Aquarian experience for humanity, every member of the group should be equal. There should be no leaders surrounded by lesser beings. The leader is usually, in that context, someone who can facilitate, or someone who can organize rather better than others, or someone who has a clearer vision or understanding of the role of the group. As for leadership *per se*, it is an old and dying concept. How should the leader make his leadership effective in the group work? By disappearing as the leader.

Competition versus Co-operation

The Master says that the people in the world can be divided into two groups: those who compete and those who co-operate. Is this division not too strict? Haven't we all both types of attitude in ourselves? Does it not depend on the situation we are in?

Of course the answer to that is yes, but it does not mean that the Master's division is too strict. It means that we all have both types of attitude in ourselves, depending on the situation. If we are in a favourable situation we will be as competitive as we are allowed to be. If we are in another situation, we will be as co-operative as we feel we need to be — at least just the minimum we can get away with. To be honest, that is how most groups work.

Everyone is both competitive and slightly co-operative, alternately. It is not as if competition becomes co-operation; it cannot. They are two opposites, and co-operation can never become competition. It is simply that the mode of response to any situation becomes the lever which you bring into play. If you must, you will be co-operative. If you can get away with it, you will be competitive, until somebody says: "No, that is too competitive. We are not having it."

It is the human psyche which is trying to dominate every situation. Some people handle all situations in a devious way, manipulating stealthily behind the scenes, getting an ally here and an ally there to back them up. All groups have this kind of activity because all this is human. That is how the bulk of humanity live — by the demonstration of the personality. Everyone is a personality; everyone is working through the personality, more or less.

The problems come out of the personality, the misuse of this manipulative aspect by the personality. That is the quality that you generally see in groups. From time to time the other qualities demonstrate, depending on whom you are dealing with. These are things which you will recognize, and you should recognize, in yourself.

I do not mean that all are manipulative, but those of you who have 3rd-ray minds and 3rd-ray brains, watch out for your manipulation! I am not saying change it, frustrate yourself, but just keep your eye on what you are actually doing, and in that way you can become detached from it. You can only detach from something if you observe it, recognize it. If you observe it without trying to change it, without justifying it, without rationalization, just simply looking at it, you will find that you become more detached. This is true for every glamour.

We all have both competition and the possibility of co-operation, because as souls we are instinctively co-operative. It is the nature of the soul to want to co-operate. It has a broad, generalized, inclusive view of life, which can only be expressed in co-operation. The thing to remember is that, in the New Age now beginning, the energy of synthesis, the energy of Aquarius itself, can only be sensed, apprehended, used, in group formation. It does not pertain to the individual but only to the group. The group needs the individual — potent, aware, intelligent, active — who can give his or her service *to the group*. Then we can act in terms of the New Age, the new Aquarian energy, that fusing, blending and synthesizing force which one day will demonstrate as the one humanity. That should be our aim.

How do we get the word out without competing with the fundamentalist religious groups?

There is no sense in competing with the fundamentalist groups. If we were competing with them we could just acknowledge we are beaten before we start. They have a Bible, the 'Word of God', they believe, hand-written by God over several centuries; they own the 'one and only' Son of God; and they have a 2,000-year start on us. Also, they command media and money.

We have a different message from these groups, or a similar message couched in different language. If you have been going out there *competing* with the fundamentalists then no wonder you got nowhere. We are not competing but giving alternative information. There is no co-operating with them, but there should be no competition. We are not converting, merely informing. Try to convert a fundamentalist!

Was it intended that some of the groups — in particular the Theosophical Society, the Arcane School, and your groups — should co-operate more closely? Or does each group have its special task that is best accomplished more or less separately, in the same sense that other disciples and groups have their own tasks in other areas such as economics and politics? (April 1998)

It would be good if the Theosophical Society, the Arcane School, and our groups could co-operate. They would have to believe what we are saying, and, unfortunately, they do not.

The Arcane School does not like our message. There is a desire for co-operation in the Geneva branch but not in London or New York. The Geneva branch is rather more open-minded, and they have said it would be very nice to work together in some way. It is difficult to find a way, because they will not say what I am saying, and I am saying what they are saying anyway. You can co-operate only with those who will co-operate. If they did, the work would go forward more quickly. However, they are still esoteric groups, and are generally no more acceptable to the media and public than we are. Every time Madame Blavatsky is mentioned by journalists, it is in a derogatory fashion. It is taken for granted that she was a fraud, and that no one today could believe her writings. It is extraordinary. After 100 years she is still not accepted as a reasonable, intelligent person, although she was a fourth-degree initiate — at the same level as Jesus of Nazareth and Leonardo da Vinci.

Were we meant to co-operate? Of course we were meant to co-operate, but you cannot co-operate with those who refuse to co-operate.

"Those who search for signs will find them"

Reports of miracles involving people of all faiths (and those of none) are increasingly reaching the world's media. According to Benjamin Creme's Master, these are all signs of the imminent emergence of Maitreya, the World Teacher, awaited by all religions under different names.

On 8 November 1977, in the 10th message Maitreya gave through Benjamin Creme, He said that His presence in the world would be accompanied by signs: "Those who search for signs will find them but My method of manifestation is more simple."

In June 1988, Maitreya's associate intimated that signs of Maitreya's presence would increase: "He is going to flood the world with such happenings that the mind can never comprehend it."

Life magazine's cover, in July 1991, asked: "Do you believe in miracles?" and reported that thousands of unexplained miraculous phenomena are occurring worldwide. "I did a little digging," said editor Peter Bonventre, "and it turned out there'd been a rash of sacred apparitions all over the world ... There's a worldwide spiritual revival, and it's one of the great stories of our time."

In April 1995, *Time* magazine devoted an eight-page spread to its cover-story on miracles, and concluded: "People are hungry for signs."

Media reports of miracles include religious statues and icons weeping tears, real blood and even pearls; the extraordinary Hindu 'milk-drinking' statues; many appearances or sightings of the Madonna; holy messages in fruit and vegetables; sweet-scented healing oil weeping from icons and paintings; spectacular coloured lights in the sky; hundreds of 'crosses of light' in windows, and 'circles of light' on buildings worldwide; miraculous healing waters and numerous reports of rescues and encounters with 'angels'.

Over recent years *Share International* magazine has reported increasing numbers of miracles around the world as Maitreya's emergence draws closer. One exceptional miracle is the manifested hand of Maitreya on a mirror in Spain in September 2001.

Job Mutungi, editor of the *Kenya Times*, witnessed Maitreya's miraculous appearance in Nairobi: "The tall figure of a bare-footed, white-robed and bearded man appeared from nowhere and stood in the middle of the crowd...Everyone was murmuring something. People were flat on the ground, weeping uncontrollably in praise and worship, in total submission to the occasion...In clear Swahili, which had no trace of accent, the strange man announced that the people of Kenya were blessed..."

Maitreya miraculously appeared 'out of the blue' to 6,000 people at a prayer meeting on Saturday, 11 June 1988 in Nairobi, Kenya. He spoke in Swahili for 15 minutes, then disappeared, leaving dozens miraculously cured of their ailments. Photographs of the event were carried by media around the world.

The approach of Maitreya

I come before you as a simple man.
I come as a Brother and Friend.
I shall return you to your Source.
I am among you till the end of the Age.
My Love surrounds you always.
My Heart beats in rhythm with yours.
My Hand shall guide you and protect you.
My Love has no bounds.

(From Message No. 90
Messages from Maitreya the Christ)

The hand of Maitreya

The photograph on the right shows the latest, extraordinary, miracle: the handprint of Maitreya Himself, miraculously manifested on a bathroom mirror in Barcelona, Spain. It is not a simple handprint but a three-dimensional image with 'photographic' detail.

First published in *Share International* magazine (October 2001), the 'hand' is a means of invoking the healing energies and help of Maitreya. By placing your hand over the photograph, or simply looking at it, Maitreya's healing and help can be invoked (subject to Karmic Law). Until Maitreya emerges fully, and we see His face, it is the closest He can come to us.

Horacio Londner

Overshadowing of Benjamin Creme by Maitreya

At the beginning and end of every lecture Benjamin Creme is overshadowed by Maitreya for about 20 to 40 minutes. In this way Maitreya releases His energy to the audience as a special spiritual nourishment or blessing. Many people who have some degree of clairvoyance have seen this energy and commented on it, but until now we have not had a photograph of the event.

This photograph was taken on 26 September 2001 in Amsterdam, Holland, at Benjamin Creme's lecture. The photographer, Ellen Bernards, was sitting in the front row on the left of the hall and took the photograph just as the initial overshadowing by Maitreya was beginning.

When the photograph was developed she noticed that instead of two people on the platform—Mr Creme and his translator Gerard Aartsen—there are three figures. Mr Creme, wearing a jacket and tie, is facing the audience, whereas the mysterious figure is facing the camera and, incidentally, has no tie and the first few buttons of His tunic are open.

The vagueness of the figures is caused by the light emanating from Maitreya during the overshadowing. Many people, for instance, see Mr Creme literally disappear behind the light.

(Benjamin Creme's Master confirms that the third figure is Maitreya.)

Hoang Van Hao

In many countries statues and icons of Jesus and the Madonna are seen to weep tears, blood and oil, and even to move. This Madonna statue from Adelaide, Australia, began weeping tears of blood in December 1992.

Over four days in September 1995, sacred Hindu statues around the world 'drank' milk offerings. Millions witnessed the milk dematerialize in this extraordinary global phenomenon.

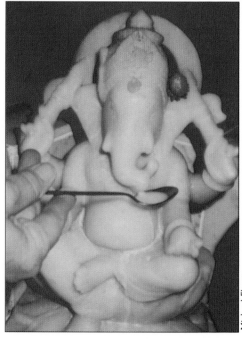

Michael Flaum

Hundreds of 'crosses of light' have been appearing in windows worldwide since first reported in 1988 in El Monte, California, USA. Many healings, both physical and emotional, are associated with the crosses.

Frances Oman

McNair Ezzard

Dramatic 'circles of light' have been appearing on buildings, pavements and other surfaces, reflected when the sun shines. *Share International* is receiving increasing numbers of photographs of 'circles of light' taken from around the world.

PART TWO

THE PROBLEM OF GLAMOUR

GLAMOUR

By the Master —, through Benjamin Creme

Of all the problems which beset humanity there is none greater than the problem of glamour. It provides the basis for all our difficulties and dangers, and holds the vast majority of humanity in thrall. It is at the root of every division and cleavage and the source of every dimension of pain and suffering. It has its roots in the ancient past of mankind and all but a very few are held under its sway.

Essentially, glamour originates in man's sensuous, feeling apparatus — the emotional or astral body — and in man's identification with its action. Through wrong identification with his feelings and emotions — his desire nature — he has surrounded himself with, and lost himself in, thick fogs of illusion and unreality. This constitutes the glamour in which most people live out their lives. Glamour is illusion on the plane of the emotions and provides the greatest obstacle to progress, for the individual and for the race. It throws a multitude of misconceptions across the path of the unwary, and the loftiest idealist is no freer from its influence (nay, he is frequently more prone) than the hardened cynic.

To come to grips with glamour, humanity must recognize its mechanism, by which means the central heresy — that we are separate — is created and maintained. All that tends to reinforce the sense of separateness is the result of the action of glamour, and all that seeks to undermine that heresy works for its destruction. Glamour resides in the notion that man's desires are real, that they have their own intrinsic validity and purpose, whereas, in truth, they are the cause of all unhappiness; no more real, no less transient, than the mirage of the desert.

The well-meaning aspirant clouds his action with desire for achievement; the idealist looks upon his as the only possible ideal that right-thinking people could hold; often do we see the absurdities of national pride lead nations into actions against the interest of their peoples. These, the actions of glamour, are the product of desire: for power and the fulfilment of ambition. The light of science has rid the world of certain ancient glamours but created others in their stead: the glamour of possessions enthrals half the world while the other half go hungry and die in misery and want.

Eventually, humanity will work through this phase and establish a truer perception of reality. The myriad glamours which beset the race today will one day dissolve in the light of man's soul, invoked into manifestation as the New Age proceeds. But the present is a time in which new types of energy are making their impact on men's lives and creating conditions of bewilderment and confusion. The heightened tension of the time fosters the glamours of fear and destruction, erupting into violence of all kinds.

What can be done to free humanity from this ancient thraldom, in part innate in the nature of substance itself? How can man free himself from wrong identification and the tyranny of his self-created thoughtforms? The answer lies in a shift of focus, from the self to the group; in a truer identification with the soul and its relation to all souls. The light of the soul, through the agency of mind, is the great dissipator of glamour, and long ago the Buddha taught the conquering of desire: the Noble Middle Path between the pairs of opposites. In the light of the soul the essential unity is seen, the astral waves subside and the aspirant finds himself at initiation's gate. (April 1984)

THE PROBLEM OF GLAMOUR

[The following article is an edited version of the keynote talk given by Benjamin Creme at the Transmission Meditation Conference in San Francisco, USA, in July 1999.]

The problem with glamour is that when we are in it we do not see it. We are totally unaware of the glamorous nature of the actions we perform. This is the eternal difficulty in dealing with glamour: you have to be outside it, above it, to see it. When you are in it, you are simply seeing your own emotional responses but not recognizing them for what they are, nor the destructive nature of these glamours.

After 17 years of these conferences and 20 years of my visits to the USA, it is still necessary to talk about the most ordinary, straightforward, simple glamours that you would expect people to recognize for themselves but which somehow they do not. So I think it is worthwhile to address, once again, this engrossing, but from the point of view of the evolution of humanity very destructive, problem.

Some groups respond more and better to their souls and are therefore, from the long-term, esoteric point of view, of greater value to the work of Hierarchy. Others work more from the personality level. Although they may be satisfied with that level, and it is useful, from the point of view of the Masters it is not the most important action that a group of this kind could be involved in.

Impatience — a major glamour

A wave of powerful energies is driving out the impurities in each person. This process finds all the hidden glamours and brings them into the open. Thus in many of the groups working for the Reappearance a rash of glamours has come to the fore.

For some people the wait for Maitreya to emerge has been too long. They become angry, impatient, disillusioned, discouraged, alienated, cynical, frustrated, bitter, disaffected. In a word, they have lost faith, which in their case is rooted in their emotional aspiration rather than their soul intuition. They experience a burnout and look for someone to blame (usually me). They should take time out and restore their nervous system.

There are also people with 'idealistic personas'. That is, they are acting a part, an idealistic notion of themselves, which gradually becomes uncomfortable because basically it is not true. This leads to the expression of the glamours of anger, even hatred, of those who have influenced and inspired them in the past. They forget how and why they came into the work.

There is the glamour of size in organizations. I call this the glamour of organization versus organism. There is a tendency in all institutions and organizations to try to get bigger, more widespread, more influential. That is a powerful glamour. In the commercial field, in large corporations, it is a glamour, but it is the glamorous nature of a large corporation to get bigger, richer and more powerful in its own field. That is not the aim, nor should it be the tendency, of an esoteric or occult group.

The ultimate role of these groups is in group initiation.[1] The four basic requirements of group initiation have not even begun to be implemented in the groups around the world: non-sentimental group relationship; working with the forces of destruction in a constructive way; working as a mini-hierarchy; and cultivating the potency of occult silence.[2] These are the absolutely fundamental requirements for group initiation, which is the underlying purpose of this grouping of groups. It has been the long-sought hope of Hierarchy to create a group that would respond to the magnetic force of a great idea, and to work under

73

the inspiration and guidance of the Masters in such a way that They could create the conditions for group initiation for the first time in 18 million years.

The glamour of organization

It is not happening, partly because of the glamour of size. It is nothing to do with size. It is nothing to do with getting bigger and bigger, more and more influential, its outreach spreading around the world, becoming the tutors of the leaders of nations. The leaders of nations are not, for the most part, the slightest bit interested in the Reappearance of the Christ. They will be, but when they are, they will not look to us for their instruction. They will look directly to the Masters, Who will be openly present — above all, to Maitreya.

The Master Djwhal Khul has written about the dangers that face every esoteric group which begins to misread its destiny, and gathers a strength on the physical plane that begins to colour its every act. It replaces the *organism* of the occult group with the *organization* of the outer groups in the world, the kind of groups which act under the aegis of a political idea, a financial or commercial theory. That has nothing to do with the esoteric group which this is.

A true esoteric or occult group is brought together under certain powerful impulses: soul impulse and intention; Hierarchical necessity; and karmic law. The idea of creating an *organization* that will be influential and powerful in the world is pure glamour. The work of preparation for the externalization of the Hierarchy is the real work of these groups around the world (whether they are given a name or, preferably, not). As soon as you name a group you give it a form, a structure, and that structure or organization which relates to the name begins to take over the destiny of the group.

The group has its own innate organic form if it is a true esoteric group. That form, and therefore the group's work, is distorted if too great an emphasis is placed on the formal, organizational aspect of its work. There are individuals in all groups, in different parts of the world, who are more inclined to the physical-plane organization of the activity. Of course, you need some degree of organization, but this can swamp the inner purposes of the group: preparing the way for the reappearance of the Christ; the return to the world of the Masters; the externalization of Their work; the education of humanity; the preparation of humanity and the groups themselves for that work; and, above all, group initiation.

The rocks of organization

The Master Djwhal Khul has written of the danger of the organization having too great an emphasis in the work of the group. He uses the example of the Theosophical Society and certain other esoteric groups which, He said, 'foundered on the rocks of organization'. I am speaking of this today because I see the same dangers becoming apparent in the work of the Reappearance groups with which I am connected in different parts of the world. I personally am concerned and I am also determined that these groups do not founder on the rocks of organization. It is not up to me entirely because one person cannot forever guide a large grouping of people in such a way that they do not founder on those rocks. We have to keep our eyes, ears, and above all our minds open to this danger — see it as a danger preferably before the danger occurs. It is better to avoid the rocks altogether than to start saving the people once they have landed on them.

It is very important for the groups everywhere to recognize this glamour of size — the glamour of the internet, the glamour of aggrandizement, of organization. Organization is necessary

75

and useful, but organization in place of *the destined activity of the group* is nothing but glamour. We have to get our priorities right.

Glamour and evolution

We are really talking about evolution when we talk about glamour. Glamour is the biggest obstacle to evolution. Evolution is mainly the building-in of good character traits. The disciple must have certain qualities if he or she is going to evolve and eventually become a Master, which is the destiny of everyone in this room. The only question is when — sooner or later?

The disciple must, above all, have courage, steadfastness, patience, the ability to 'stay there' and not run away from difficulties which have been placed before us to bring out the best in us. We meet these difficulties in life because the soul arranges it in such a way that when we overcome them we have progress; we have taken a step forward in our evolutionary journey. The disciple also needs humility and simplicity.

We need the ability, probably above all, to renounce the lower for the higher, which is the Law of Sacrifice. This leads naturally to right detachment. Wrong detachment (isolation) is the result of rationalization of faults and rejection of criticism, even if constructive and from a Master, and is a major and self-destructive glamour. The inability to take constructive criticism, even if it stems from a Master, is one of the major glamours which halts the journey to perfection of countless individuals. It is rationalization by the mind, and this maintains the glamour. A person is told their chief glamour is such and such, and they do not like that. No one likes to be told of any glamour, let alone a major glamour. As soon as they hear it, they say: "That is not true," or "That is the opposite of what I am." Usually our sense of ourselves is the opposite of reality.

What we take to be our major achievement is often our major glamour. The Master Djwhal Khul spoke about this very humbly when He revealed how His major glamour, which had kept Him back for a long time, was His devotion to His Master. Devotion is a good thing, you would think, especially of a pupil to a Master. He was a disciple of the Master Koot Hoomi but that devotion literally held Him back.

That is how glamour works. It is a fog, an illusion. It is seeing the opposite of what is true — not being able to see the truth because of the fog of one's emotional responses. Devotion can sustain those at the early stage of being a disciple, but not when you get to the point where the Master Djwhal Khul was at that time, when He was aware of, and worked with, His Master. Sooner or later devotion has to give way to knowledge.

Awakening to our glamours

We have to become aware of what glamour is and what it is not. Glamour is anything that hides the truth from our experience. Are we seeing reality? If so, there is no glamour involved. Or are we seeing reality through a fog of illusion? Most people — anyone who is not yet half-way between the first and second initiation — are seeing reality to some degree through glamour. Once the step beyond 1.5 to 1.6 is taken, the polarization shifts from astral (the seat of consciousness of the vast majority of people) to mental polarization. Over 90 per cent of all people are astrally polarized and therefore subject to glamour.

Once you take the first initiation, you begin to awaken to the glamours. You will go on having them. You will go on being as blind as you ever were in finding your way through the labyrinth. But gradually you will see that it is a labyrinth, that there are doors leading nowhere. Gradually a light will start to descend as you progress and make more and more contact with your own soul — through service and meditation, above all Transmission Meditation.

The light of the soul, working through the mental body, sooner or later throws a light on the glamour. You can begin, through the mind, to look at a situation and recognize the glamour of your response. Before that you could not see it because you were in it, totally. The darkness begins to thin and gradually you see that you are living in a very uncomfortable way. You are doing things which you know, more and more, are unreal. You suddenly see that your beliefs are not worth having. They are not real. They are simply glamour, covering something else. What is that something else?

You look, and you throw the light of the soul, through the mental body, on the situation. As you progress, as you become more mentally polarized, a time comes when the soul-light begins to dissipate the glamours. When it does, a new world is shown to you, and that new world is yourself. You begin to see that you can act more directly, more spontaneously, more truly, more honestly, with greater sincerity and detachment than you have ever done before. This shows the movement from astral polarization to mental polarization, and takes you up to 2.5-2.6. Then again there is a shift, and suddenly what was illusion (glamour on the mental plane), without your noticing it, becomes clear and simple. There is a direct intuitive understanding from your soul infusing every action, every situation in which you are engaged. This is the light of the soul which results from your spiritual polarization. That is the aim for everyone, and everyone has to go through this same process.

The fact that people have glamour is not something to be proud of, but neither is it a crime. If it were, everyone would be a criminal in that sense. Everyone has the deficiency of glamour in their action, in their make-up, and in their sense of reality. It is the source of all the sins and all the pain in the world, because essentially it is to do with wrong identification. We identify with what is, literally, unreal.

The destructive glamour of criticism

A major problem for leaders of groups is to withstand the often concentrated (even if unvoiced) criticism from those they lead. This happens at every level from small groups to leaders of nations. The Master Djwhal Khul states it as follows:

"Leaders of men, whether of groups, communities, or nations, are particularly subject to criticism by those they are leading and serving. This refers to the genuine leaders whose primary objective it is to serve the interests of those they represent or those who have been placed under their charge. Such leaders should constantly be supported by the energy of 'loving understanding', but instead they are so often badly handicapped by criticism accentuating all their imperfections. Such criticism often results in seriously crippling the leader's effective service. So often this criticism is rooted in jealousy, thwarted ambition or pride of intellect. It is so easy to sit in judgement of the leader and to criticize him with regard to action or non-action for which the critic does not carry the responsibility, and neither is he, as a rule, fully aware of all the relevant facts and their implications. Such destructive criticism is harmful to both the critic and the criticized leader.

"Group leaders are often subject to streams of poisonous thoughts, to idle gossip of a destructive nature, and to jealousies, hates and frustrated ambitions of members who would like to see their leader superseded. As may be expected this must have an adverse affect on the leader, and might produce both physical and emotional effects; the more evolved the leader the greater will be his sensitivity and the more acute will be the pain and suffering that is inflicted. All the leader can do in such circumstances is to withdraw within himself, to guard

against all signs of bitterness and self pity which will be inclined to arise, and with loving understanding to wait for the time when the members come to their senses, arrive at clearer insight, and learn to co-operate with a spirit of goodwill.

"Group members should also realize that criticism of any kind can only create disturbed relationships within the ranks of the group, thereby undermining the effectiveness of the group as a whole, delaying the progress of the work and enervating its quality." (From: Aart Jurriaanse, *Bridges,* p378.)

Mass glamour

If ever there was an illustration of organized mass glamour, it was the attack by the Republican Party on President Clinton, who at the time was trying to deal with major political and other issues in the world. He was attacked, ridiculed and humiliated to a degree that has not happened before in my memory. I have never, anywhere, seen such an attack, such an exposé of little offences, which, if they had happened in France, for example, would have caused laughter in every bistro. An ex-President of France was known by all the French and half of Europe to have had an extra-marital liaison with a woman for 30 or 40 years. He went around with the child of that liaison known to the people of France.

The American public, out of this glamour, this combination of obsession with sex and at the same time total fear of sex, attacked and humiliated the President, to their shame. He is not above being attacked, but he should be attacked, if necessary, for what he is responsible for, which is the wellbeing of the people, the political and economic system, and the country's relation to other nations. That is the basis on which the President should be judged. The humiliation, the extraordinary attack on him, which must have made it difficult, so altogether grievous, in his relation to other leaders with whom he had to meet and deal at the same time — that was ugly and utterly unfair.

That is mass glamour, but of course for political reasons. That is how political groups act, but the same glamour exists in many other groups, including the so-called spiritual. The political groups in this country (USA) lead a life of their own because the political system is basically, fundamentally, corrupt. The corruption is endemic. It allows one party, as soon as someone from the other party is elected President, immediately to smear everything that he does. The attempt is to show his basic corruption, as every politician in this country is said to be corrupt, and so show his unfitness for office.

That is mass glamour of a kind which I think the American people should take very seriously indeed. Now that it is over, the tendency will be to forget it. It will happen again and again. Whoever is elected President at the next election will within six months be accused of fraud, sexual and all kinds of misdemeanours which would slacken his hold on the Presidency and perhaps let the other side in. At the same time it breaks down the democracy of the country. They do not accept that when a President is elected, of whatever party, it is the will of the people; otherwise it probably would not happen. You corrupt the system if you do not accept that. As soon as the President is in, the other party tries every dirty trick to get rid of him — therefore acting against the will of the people. With Maitreya and the Masters coming out into the world it may be that this will disappear. I hope so, but it will only disappear if you, the citizens of the USA, make it disappear. That is glamour on a national scale.

Control of speech

The forming of cliques within a group is extremely harmful. It shows a separative spirit which is the very opposite of group consciousness. If people were more self-disciplined, and above all controlled their speech, they would create better group relations.

One of the most corrosive of all astral glamours is gossip. Gossip is very harmful in a group. For many people, gossip is the very staff of life (more important than bread and water!). There are types who cannot live without gossip. The problem is that they do not recognize gossip for what it is. They rationalize their desire for gossip into simply the exchange of information or everyday communication of news from one human to another. Therefore they see no harm in it. But gossip knows no boundaries. It goes all the way from innocent spreading of information, positive or negative, to a systematic breakdown of group trust and therefore group relationship — jumping to conclusions, rash judgements on insufficient knowledge, condemnation, and therefore polarization of the group. If any individual in a group achieves some upward step, some achievement in the expression of themselves as a soul, it is an achievement not only for that person, but for each individual in the group and for the group as a whole.

These achievements may take subtle forms. Others may be obvious, outer things — for example, meeting in one form or another with Maitreya. No one knows the underlying reason why some people have an experience with Maitreya. Some people either do not have an experience or do not remember having had an experience. More people have had experiences than ever make them known. Also, the experiences continue unabated. Most days of the week bring letters of these extraordinary meetings: funny, sad, solemn, hilarious, caring and deeply touching, they run the gamut of human situations like a series of characters in a play. In these different ways, Maitreya (or a Master) confirms the reality of Their presence — even as only 'familiars' — and console, teach and inspire according to need. They should be a source of joy for everyone involved in this work. (*Share International,* January/February 2000.)

[1]   For more information on group initiation, read Benjamin Creme, *Maitreya's Mission,, Volume Two*, Chapter 19, 'Towards Group Initiation'.

[2] See Alice A. Bailey, *The Rays and the Initiations*, Rule XI.

I am among you once more, My dear friends.
I come to tell you that you will see Me very soon, each in his own way.

Those who look for Me in terms of My Beloved Disciple, the Master Jesus, will find His qualities in Me.
Those who look for Me as a Teacher are nearer the mark, for that is what I am.
Those who search for signs will find them, but My method of manifestation is more simple.

Nothing separates you from Me, and soon many will realize this.
I am with you and in you.
I seek to express That which I am through you;
for this I come.

Many will follow Me and see Me as their Guide.
Many will know Me not.
My aim is to enter into the life of all men and through them change that life.
Be ready to see Me soon.
Be ready to hear My words,
to follow My thoughts,
to heed My Plea.

I am the Stranger at the Gate.
I am the One Who knocks.
I am the One Who will not go away.

I am your Friend.
I am your Hope.
I am your Shield.
I am your Love.
I am All in All.

Take Me into yourselves, and let Me work through you.
Make Me part of yourselves, and show Me to the world.
Allow Me to manifest through you, and know God.

From Message No. 10 – 8 November 1977

THE PROBLEM OF GLAMOUR

QUESTIONS AND ANSWERS

*[Questions without publication date are from the 1999 conferences in the USA and Japan and were published in **Share International** January/February 2000. Questions marked 'JC' are from Benjamin Creme's Japanese Conference in 2000, and so far unpublished.]*

Organism versus Organization

When does the organism lose its balance and become an organization? Is it a case of preoccupation with form?

It certainly has to do with preoccupation with form, because it is much easier to create an organization than to create and maintain an organism. They are two different things.

When does the organism lose its balance? It is not a question of the organism losing its balance, it is the result of a change of direction in purpose. When the first group was formed in London in 1974, my Master said to me: "Bring together these people and form the group." (He had given me names of certain people.) He said: "Do not call it anything. Do not give it a name. Do not have officers, no chairman, no secretary, no one with any office at all." And he said: "Do not construct around yourselves a fence separating you from other groups but do not affiliate yourself with any other group." We are standing in a very special position in this activity related to the activity of other groups, because the whole world is really involved at some level in the reappearance of the Christ whether they know it or not; the Masters are training people at all different levels. There is the New Group of World Servers to which members of many groups would claim to belong. Some of them do and many of them do not.

So why these requirements? There should be no officers so that there would be no one *in charge*, no one whose word would be taken as the only arbiter in the group. There should be no chairman (who would naturally be me because I formed the group and was in touch with the Master), whose word would dominate the ideas of the other members. There should be no secretary who would automatically deal with the day-to-day running of the group and thus come into a powerful position. And we should not put a fence around ourselves and say: "This is what we believe and you do not."

These requirements are followed to avoid the creation of a separatist approach to this work of the Externalization of the Hierarchy. That enabled us, at least in London, to make, and maintain, an organism. Elsewhere, organizations have been formed, for various reasons, with boards of directors to run things, but in London, the initial organism has no board. No one is in charge. Everyone has the same relationship to everyone else. Obviously, since I am in touch with the Master, have had certain experiences, created the group in the first place and introduced Transmission Meditation, I became the natural leader of the group. My word is taken seriously, and that is natural. That is the recognition that there are different levels of experience, awareness, and knowledge as a result of that experience. Since I could at any moment talk to the Master and ask Him for advice if He wished to give it on any problem arising in the group, this became the norm. The group really functioned, and still functions, as an organism, a group.

I have never forgotten what the Master Djwhal Khul said, writing about the Theosophical Society and other societies: "They foundered on the rocks of organization." As soon as Madame Blavatsky died, the form of the group changed. People like Judge and Olcott took over the organization and made it such a rigid structure that it could no longer breathe. Eventually, people like Alice Bailey, who worked at the Theosophical Society in New York with her husband and some friends, wanted a more democratic, looser, more organic structure. They became too 'dangerous' and were thrown out on the street.

In the Theosophical Society, the soul-aspect of Madame Blavatsky was not involved. Rather, it was her personality alone which guided. She was a fourth-degree initiate, and had a potent and high-powered personality informed by a 1st-ray soul. She was a very powerful being, which you have to be to found such a society, to have the courage and strength to bring all these new ideas into the world against the scornful reaction from all the scientific, philosophical, sociological, religious, and psychological groups of that time.

The Theosophical Society foundered on the actions of those who took charge after she died because her soul was not involved and had never been. Her personality influence did not for long outlast her death and the society became over-organized and crystallized. When Alice Bailey tried to structure the society in a more organic, democratic and meaningful way, many people objected, especially in this country [USA]. For two years, Annie Besant, the president at the time, supported her. But even Annie Besant could not support her indefinitely.

In order to be an organism, a group must be inclusive. There should not be officers, those who run it. There should be a mutual involvement of interested and dedicated people working impersonally for the good of the whole and therefore of the world.

Given that Madame Blavatsky was a senior disciple, how is it possible that she sometimes worked only or largely from the personality level? Is the soul input not automatic after the third initiation?

She was a 4rth-degree initiate. Her soul, therefore, was reabsorbed into the Monad. Her *soul-infused* personality was, consequently, the agency for her work.

Greater outreach naturally results in a bigger organization, so what is the problem?

There speaks the organizational man. Greater outreach can work in different ways. It can work for the organization and make it more widespread: you need to employ more people, give more time to the organizational aspects rather than the productive aspects if it is something that you make or sell around the world. But in an organism, a grouping of groups which this is, the problem is that as you make the outreach, more and more time and energy is devoted to the growing organization; by its very nature it becomes the be-all and end-all of the work of the group. This group is working in several ways. It is trying to make a wide but not necessarily the widest possible outreach. I could have arrived at the widest possible outreach many years ago if I had used public relations firms. Everyone that we could have possibly reached would now have been reached. Outreach would be maximum, but it would have required an elaborate organization to maintain and oversee which would be the work of many people. That would take over from the actual work of preparing humanity for the Reappearance.

The problem is not so much a question of balance but rather of recognizing the limitations on a group like this which is projecting an idea rather than selling a product. That would be trying to use a commercial practice, which commercialization has developed to absolute perfection, in a situation which is not to do with commerce. We are trying to change consciousness, so you approach that in a completely different way. To say that you want greater outreach is true, but you do not need maximum outreach. If you want to influence 100 people, perhaps you only need to influence 10 people. Then those 10 people influence others until there is a mass of people whom you have not necessarily reached directly but have reached through others.

When my Master told me to go out and tell this information to the world, I asked: "How do I start?" He said: "Write to the groups." I said: "Which groups?" He said: "Any groups." I was not connected with any group. He said: "Any group, all groups, of all backgrounds, teachings, traditions, all of them, any of them." He said: "Reach the groups. Write to the groups. Offer your services as a speaker on the Reappearance in line with the Alice Bailey and Theosophical teachings," which eventually I did. I got a pamphlet with a list of groups and sent off to every one of them, about 50 in all.

The Master said: "If you get to the minds of the groups, from these groups will go out a telepathic interplay with the mass of people, so that when you go to the public they will be already somewhat informed by the thoughtforms created by the groups who have more focused minds than the masses."

So I did this, but I received only six replies. Three of them were: "Thank you very much but we have our own speakers." Or: "We are booked up for the next three years, but we will be happy to put you on a list of possible speakers." Or: "What are the Alice Bailey teachings?" Only three were positive in the sense that they invited me for a meeting to come and discuss my ideas. And so I began talking. Out of perhaps 50, only these three were of any value at all, but I was able to start.

You start in a small way and it just grows and grows. It grows because people say: "I was at a meeting the other night. There were 30 people there, and I heard the most extraordinary information. Maybe we could have him speak to us too." And they started inviting me. One person tells 20 and they tell 40 and they tell 100. You do not have to get to every individual. You do not need a massive organization for the greatest possible outreach. What you do is what I try to do, use the media — get on radio and television if possible, give interviews. That way you reach thousands sometimes hundreds of thousands, occasionally millions of people. There are people in this country who heard me speak back in 1981. It is nearly 20 years ago but they have the feeling that it was just a few years ago. They remember it; no one forgets this story. The story is so potent, so unusual, so different from all other information that, if they are open, it stays in the memory. That is all you need to do. You do not need a huge organization to do that. We did not have a huge organization when I first came to America. There was no organization of any kind, but there was a group of interested people, and that started the work in America.

As for Tara Center or Share International Foundation, there was, in the beginning, a necessity to form organizations in order to publish books, magazines, etc. If they could simply have remained as the provider (publisher) of the books and informational material, and/or focus their attention on promoting your media interviews, would this meet the requirements?

It is a question of seeing what is needed. If you are well-organized in the right way, you know already. Tara Center has a mechanism of approach to the media (although it gets more and more difficult as the media become more and more self-protective). Nevertheless, there are more radio interviews, occasionally television and newspaper interviews, in America than anywhere else in the world. There is more media here. There are more radio stations, every small town has one. There are more networks of stations; you speak to one station and that is broadcast to a number of states. That must inform millions of people in this country. You do not need a huge organization to do that. You just need a liaison between the group and the media, and the group and me.

If the same thing pertained in all the countries I would be worked off my feet but that same saturation of ideas could take place in Europe and elsewhere. The one place in Europe where we really get a lot of media attention is Spain. For that reason Spain is extremely successful in making the information known. The groups also use a large percentage of soul energy, and lecture widely and often. They have built up a good connection with various media; a pleasant, personal relationship between members of the group and interested journalists, so that every time I go to Madrid or Barcelona or wherever, they will want to interview me. There is an ongoing memory of what went before. I go there once a year, so that people are kept informed in a repetitive way. Hearing it again and again is important. For that you do not need a huge organization. You just need people with the talent, the nerve, perseverance and diplomacy to approach and work with the media.

I'm confused: the groups working with you are supposed to be democratic and yet in each country there seems to be a centre. Wouldn't it be better to have no centre and be completely decentralized? Why are there centres: like London for UK, Tara Center in USA, Amsterdam in Holland or Christchurch in New Zealand? (July/August 2000)

The centres have evolved naturally in relation to the activity of the co-workers. This activity sets up a magnetic, attractive force and helps the spreading of the information — the message. As more and more groups are formed, a centre is necessary to co-ordinate their work somewhat, which co-ordination adds strength and effectiveness to the work. With *goodwill* and *mutual co-operation* there is no reason at all why the democratic

91

process should be infringed. I am not suggesting that all groups actually function in a fully democratic way — personality defects in individuals often prevent that — but that is the ideal which, to my mind, is perfectly attainable in time.

The Master Djwhal Khul, when talking about group problems and the 'failure' of the group experiment with a group of disciples as described in Discipleship in the New Age, Volumes I & II *(Alice A.Bailey), writes that one of the main contributory factors in the lack of success was the 'inactivity of the heart'. Could you explain what He meant and how does this happen in a group of aspirants which one might expect to be motivated by the action of their hearts?*

The relative success or failure of an esoteric group is measured by the degree to which the soul involvement — and therefore the 'activity of the heart' — is high, and the degree to which the personality — and therefore the 'inactivity of the heart' — is uppermost.

It is a matter of the glamours of the personality preventing the expression of soul wisdom and insight. It is possible for a Master to measure with great accuracy which groups working for the Reappearance, for example, fit into one or other category. The groups have been informed where they stand in this respect, and know, therefore, the direction in which they must move if they wish to be considered 'successful' in their task.

Focusing on the Priorities

What do you think is more effective: giving talks to quite small — or even very small — audiences, or putting the story out on the internet where a huge audience can see it?

I haven't the slightest hesitation in saying that live talks, like live television interviews, are far more effective than the written word, whether on the internet or elsewhere. There is an energy communication in a talk which convinces of itself. To bear witness is to invoke that energy. If you ask an audience (many groups do at my lectures) what, among many sources (radio or newspaper ads, flyers, word of mouth, etc), brought them there, the most often quoted is, inevitably, 'word of mouth'. Their friends' recommendation is the result of hearing a talk and inspires them to pass it on. The internet is useful, especially to interested journalists, but not nearly as effective or convincing as the spoken word with all one's conviction behind it.

Is there a wrong kind of service?

Yes. There is a major glamour going on in several groups at the present time — the misuse of the short time left in preparing the way for the reappearance of the Christ. We all know that teaching the world about the fact of the Reappearance and the emergence of Hierarchy is the priority. That is real service; that is tough, difficult. For that you need courage. There is a much easier 'service' — more relaxed, nicer, but still interesting for those participating — which is talking about the rays for example: the rays of one's country, one's city, their interrelation with other rays and other cities, why we have trade relations or not. People spend a lot of time and energy on these non-priorities. It is pure glamour. They write to me for answers to a host of questions which would elucidate further for their listeners a whole new knowledge of the rays. They would like to talk about them but they do not know the answers, so they write to me. I do not even take the trouble to reply because the activity itself is so misguided at this time.

Why are they not putting their time and energy, in the short time that remains, into talking about the reappearance of the

Christ, the externalization of the Hierarchy, the changes that will take place in the world, preparing the world for that? Because they do not have the courage, because it is easier to talk about the rays. Rays are interesting and 'esoteric'. They make a nice show, and need quite a lot of study to talk about seriously. It is easy and fascinating to do, so people do it and fool themselves that they are serving.

It is not easy, and it may or may not be fascinating, to talk about the reappearance of the Christ, but it takes courage. It takes courage to go out and talk to people who are going to say: "This is a load of 'codswallop'. You cannot expect us to believe that." They may not say that, but they often do. It takes courage to face that, to put on a meeting in which you are talking about the reappearance of the Christ. Talking about the rays is an interesting topic, something which you can read about on your own, but it is not preparing humanity for the Reappearance.

How many people need to know about the interaction of the various rays, the virtues and vices of the rays, in order to understand that the man whom they are going to see very shortly on television is the Christ, the World Teacher, the Imam Mahdi, the Messiah, Whomever they await? They need to know that; that is preparation. Talking to groups who probably already know all about the rays is just playing at being active when you are not really being active at all. That is a major glamour today.

You have said in the past that co-workers who wanted to devote their time and energy to causes like homelessness and hunger would be more effective if they worked for the Reappearance because there are lots of homelessness and hunger groups but only one group working for the Reappearance. Is this still the case today (1999)?

Broadly speaking, yes. We are not the only group working for the Reappearance, but we are the ones who know that that is what we are doing. Many groups are working in the political field, and they do not know that they are working for the Reappearance. But they are working for the transformation of society, which is what the Reappearance is about. It is not just about the emergence of a group of men, however exalted. Since we are the only ones who are literally talking about the reappearance of the Christ and the Masters of Wisdom, about the transformation that will result, I think it is more effective to devote your time and energy to the Reappearance work. If you have lots of time and energy, you can do lots of different things. There is no reason why you cannot help the homeless and work with hunger groups while working for the Reappearance. It depends how dynamic you are.

Destructive Glamour of Criticism

You have spoken about the need to control speech, to express the proper word at the proper place and time. I have been thinking about that quite a bit. Did you mean to control speech or to control our thoughts?

What I meant about controlling speech was focused on the question of glamour and the necessity in groups for non-criticism and no gossip. Controlling speech in the sense of watching that you do not gossip. Watch that you do not talk about other people, especially behind their back, that you do not make up stories or listen to stories about other people. In other words, gossip should be totally outside the group activity.

If one says there should be no criticism, people think they understand. Criticism is harsh, and they understand they are not supposed to do it (even if they actually do). But gossip, even if it is not harsh, even if it is not terribly critical, is very dangerous because it is insidious. It destroys the relationship of trust between the members of the group. In every group there are gossips, big ones and little ones. There are always those who want to bring the latest information. They are usually people who are of little use in the group. They are just carriers of the latest 'news'. That is very dangerous because it destroys trust and leads to the creation of little groups of people who work not with the group but in cliques. That is a very separative tendency. It ultimately destroys the cohesiveness of the group or prevents the creation of that cohesion.

Glamour is something that every group has to deal with. This is so much the case that the Master Djwhal Khul wrote an entire book on it: *Glamour: A World Problem* (Lucis Trust, 1950). It is the major problem in the world. It is behind all the ills and sufferings in the world. The best thing you can do for the world is to raise your consciousness to the mental plane, become mentally polarized, and so clarify, somewhat, the general fog of glamour in the world.

Group glamour is the result of individual glamour. We are dealing with groups, so it is better to deal with glamour as it affects the group. Do not imagine that today, tomorrow or this weekend we will have solved the problems of group glamour. They are endless and will not be solved immediately — but we can make a start.

One of the most important factors in overcoming glamour is honesty, being able to use the mental plane in an honest way, so that you have honesty of mind. If you have a glamour and refuse to look at it honestly, it never goes away. But if you look at it from the mental plane, honestly, it disappears by itself. When you become aware, the glamour disappears.

Glamour is the dark, the lack of light. It is the source of all ignorance. We are supposed to be on a movement from the dark to the light, from ignorance to wisdom. That is why it is absolutely, fundamentally, important for every disciple at the beginning of their path to tackle their glamours, simply, honestly, without judgement or self-condemnation. It is seeing oneself objectively.

I think about criticism a lot. When I see myself criticizing someone else's work, I can see that I am criticizing. Is it better to express myself with criticism than to say something else that is not honest? How do I deal with that, if I am going to be honest with myself?

Honesty is a very good quality, but it should not be practised in such a way as to destroy or cause harm. When you are being honest, you are being honest only within your own parameters, your own understanding of truth, which, let us admit, is relatively limited. If you feel you have to criticize the activities or work of someone else, you should do so only in the spirit of enlightenment, or constructive criticism, not simply destructively. You have to ask yourself: "Do I have a right from where I stand to give this constructive criticism? Who am I to impose on this person my idea of what they should or should not do?"

For example, at lectures people often come to me with books. About 99.999 per cent of these books are communications from the astral planes, if they are not from the person's own subconscious. When I see the book, I know from which level it is coming. It is never from the Masters, even if the person thinks it is. If the person comes up to me and says: "This book is from the Masters. Will you accept it?", I accept it, then usually give it away. But if they ask me from what level this is coming, I will hold it and I can tell if it is coming from the astral. It is usually the fifth, occasionally the sixth, astral plane. I say it is coming from the fifth astral. They can believe it or not. But if someone says in a question: "What do you think of the book such and such by so and so?", I do not answer that question because that would just be criticism, and not constructive criticism. This is how honesty comes in. If I am asked, I am honest and say it comes from such and such. If I am not asked I say nothing. I do not hold it up and say: "Now listen everyone. This is coming from the fifth astral plane. Avoid it. It is full of rubbish. It is a nonsense." That would simply be negative criticism. It is not my role to make those public judgements.

You have to know where you stand in relation to this criticism. Do you have the right to criticize? Are the people asking for your criticism? Or are you making yourself the schoolteacher? No one is perfect; otherwise they would be Masters. I am sure you are more perfect than others in one way, and they are more perfect than you in other ways. So who has the right to criticize?

On the other hand, if Titian, Rembrandt or Leonardo da Vinci came to criticize my paintings, I would be very happy. I would be delighted to have their criticism because I would respect the level from which they were criticizing. However, if a teacher at the local art club came along criticizing, I would say: "What does he know about it?" It has to do with common sense. Most problems connected with glamour have a big constituent of common sense.

Most people in the groups are so idealistic that the very idea that they could be critical never enters their mind. "Me critical? Oh, no, I have the biggest ideals about the group." Everyone has these ideals, but they do not actually put the ideals into practice, and do not see that they do not. They say: "I do not like so and so. She is so critical." They do not see that they are criticizing. Usually, whatever you dislike most in others, whatever qualities in other people really make you angry, are the ones which you have strongest in yourself. The person in the group who thinks everyone is angry with them, everyone dislikes them, is the one who is angry with everybody, who dislikes everybody, who cannot work with others, cannot see the good in others. That is their problem.

The thing to remember is that everyone doing this work is doing it for the best of all possible reasons, because their soul has told them this is real, and that they should be involved in it. Everyone has the best intentions. They mean well. They do not necessarily *do* well, but they mean well. So you have to be more tolerant. If you are tolerant the criticism subsides.

How do we deal with criticism in group work in a constructive way? (January/February 1998)

There are two kinds of criticism — destructive and constructive. Destructive criticism is what everyone applies to everyone else. Constructive criticism is relatively rare, because you have to be in a position not only to see the break in the rhythm of an individual which makes him or her open to criticism but also to be the healer. You have to give the recommendation for its correction. That is not easy when you are dealing with other people. It is not easy when you are dealing with yourself!

In dealing with other people you have to be very sure of your ground before you can give constructive criticism. Any other kind of criticism should be abandoned, not given voice. It destroys right relationship and trust, it demeans the person who is criticized and the person who is criticizing. I know that everyone does it. There is not an individual in the world, probably, below a 4.9-degree initiate, who is not capable of this kind of criticism. But we should all eschew it as much as we can.

I believe that there are times in everyone's group activity in which criticism of a constructive kind can be useful in reorienting that person to a more correct, more consistent mode of activity. In which case everyone has to be open to this kind of constructive criticism. You will find that this is not so.

Constructive criticism is taken, almost always, as negative criticism by those who receive it, unless they are particularly, unusually, detached.

If a person is detached, they will take any amount of criticism, whether justified or unjustified, destructive or constructive; but how often do you meet a person so detached that they can take with total equilibrium, even amiability, that kind of criticism? Everyone believes that they should be treated with total respect, and in group work everyone should trust, as a matter of course, that fundamentally they have the respect of every other member of the group. That is a number one requirement: a basic, unspoken, but nevertheless recognized and felt, respect for who and what they are, and the belief that everyone is doing what they are doing honestly, to the best of their ability, and for the right reasons. It is not always true, but they have to feel that it is there.

Everyone approaches the work we are doing with mixed motives. The first motive is an awareness that this is probably the most important work (I believe *it is* the most important work) that anyone could be doing in the world today. Of course, a high-powered surgeon would think that there are other, just as important, things to do. In a relative sense that is true, but speaking in world terms, in terms of the effect on the future of the race, the externalization of the Hierarchy, and the work connected with that is, beyond question, to my mind, the most important work that anyone could be involved in.

That is why the number of people involved is relatively small, because it demands so much. If it is the most important work, it demands total dedication to it. How often do you get someone totally dedicated to something they cannot see, can only read or hear about, can only take as a possibility? That is why certain gurus in the world are followed and adored, and others, unknown, are neglected, ignored.

There is, inevitably, criticism in every group, because in every group there are mistakes. Who is to say which is a mistake and which is not simply an experiment? There is room for experiment in every activity. On the other hand, although there is no such thing as time, there is a time factor at work. There is a time to do certain work, and a time when it is too late to do that work.

You have to concentrate on the *meaningful* work at any given time. However, that is where criticism comes in, because people will disagree on what that is and how you evaluate it. When you have these differences of opinion — because of different points of view, different rays, different ways of looking at the world, different points in evolution to some little degree — different emphasis is given to different things. You have to arrive at consensus, and consensus is the result of co-operation.

Is criticism always a bad thing or is constructive criticism sometimes necessary to correct errors in group work? If so, what are the guidelines for constructive criticism?

There is such a thing as constructive criticism, and it is often essential for it to be voiced. But the requirements are rather onerous. You have to know with absolute truth that you are standing in a higher and better position in relation to the problem than the person you are criticising. If, in all honesty and without glamour, you can say that you are seeing the problem from a higher level and therefore that this is constructive criticism (not personal criticism but to do with the better functioning of the work and the group), then you certainly have a right, and even a duty, to give constructive criticism — and if you think you know all the factors involved, which you have to do in order to be constructive in your criticism. The question is: when is it constructive and when is it not? When do you have the right and when do you not? You do not have the right if your criticism is based on partiality, liking or disliking, on inferior or inadequate knowledge of the situation. All of these have to be taken into account in giving so-called constructive criticism. If you meet these requirements, then indeed, constructive criticism is possible and right.

Major Glamours of the USA

Is it possible to point out some of the major glamours of the groups in the United States?

The major glamours of the groups in the United States are the major glamours of the groups around the world. But they are coloured by the 6th-ray personality of the United States which naturally affects the ways of thinking, feeling and relating of the groups here. The glamours are not so very different from those of the Japanese, Dutch, Russian or other nations.

The United States is huge and it is young, a teenager. You have around 265 million people. In a huge nation there is a conglomeration of the same ray. If that ray is the 6th, you are going to notice it. How could you not? It built America. Can you imagine if you had first come to America and did not have a 6th ray, or weren't influenced by the 6th ray, like most American people were and still are? There would be no America. It would have died out on the outskirts of New York. Instead, the early pioneers walked or rode across the Great Plains and came to the Rocky Mountains in winter time. It surely was awful that first time. They went up and over, down the other side and got to San Francisco.

The major glamours of the US are the major glamours of the 6th ray: idealism to a fault; a vision, in this case a very materialistic vision, of a land of plenty in which there is 'abundance'. Abundance is still presented to the American people by all the commercial companies as the dream they want fulfilled. "You want abundance? We've got it and we will sell it to you." You have 'bought' the idea of abundance. There is something wrong with abundance when abundance is what you think you require. When *sufficiency* is seen as abundance, you will recognize that you have achieved that long ago.

That is the problem of the materialistic society of America today. You do not recognize that true abundance is sufficiency. The industrial revolution has made it possible for everyone to live in sufficiency. But we have the unhappy circumstance of half the world living in super-abundance and the rest in penury and dying of want.

The Master Djwhal Khul says that the world is waiting for the 2nd-ray soul of America to manifest itself, and when it does it will begin the transformation of the world. It will see sufficiency as abundance and the need to share. This glamour of abundance, which practically everyone has, is taken with your mother's milk. Every commercial that has ever been shown on television has presented a false picture of abundance. The so-called 'spiritual groups' are also smitten with this word abundance. They want abundance, and they want it now. They have no patience.

Everything worthwhile, long-lasting, needs patience. People who have been working for the Reappearance for years are beginning to lose patience. No matter the growing evidence on a daily basis that Maitreya is here, no matter what experiences they have had with Maitreya or the Master Jesus, no matter how many times they have had insights and drawn their conclusions, they have become impatient after all these years. It is a long time for people to sustain their hope. Unfortunately, for many people, especially with a 6th-ray make-up, it is hope, aspiration of an emotional kind, and not the total, inner certainty of the intuition, which drives them to work for the Reappearance. Our work is like the drop of water, dropping on the stone until gradually the stone is worn away and the hole is made. That is how it has to be. That requires patience.

Patience is something Americans, on the whole, do not have for all sorts of historical reasons. It is, in part, the opposite quality to the readiness of most Americans to 'get up and go', to do, to build a house. I have never met so many people who are not builders or even carpenters but who have built their own house. In Europe, if you can afford it, you get someone else to build a house for you. You would never start building your own house unless you were a builder, unless you had some training that would give you a start. I know people in the US, with no training whatsoever, who have built a house. You think nothing about doing it. Or driving from here to Miami, thousands of miles. We would seldom do that in Europe. If you started off in Paris and drove for 4,000 miles you would end up somewhere in Mongolia, looking around for Shamballa and not finding it anywhere!

You have a very different concept of distance and life generally from the rest of the world. That makes you interesting, but there are problems with it too, such as lack of patience. That is one of the biggest glamours — wanting it today, or tomorrow at the very latest, rather than building towards it, being patient, and fashioning it. You have to fashion the Reappearance. You have to fashion your own evolution and development. It does not just happen. You just want to 'go with the flow'. If you go with the flow nothing happens. Your interior life is not out there flowing. I think that is actually a lazy, fatalistic attitude. Many think that if they meet the right people and come under the right influences they will 'get there'. That is probably true, but who are the right people? What are the right influences? You have to be open and aware and ready to receive what you are given.

If you have read too many of the wrong books, as most 'New Agers' have, when you meet the right thing you do not recognize it. That is the problem for a lot of people. They do not recognize what they are given, for example, in the opportunity to work for the reappearance of the Christ and the Masters of Wisdom, the externalization of the Hierarchy. Can you think of anything more important to humanity, in the whole of life, than that? A time, again, when the Christ is walking among us, talking to millions of people on radio and television, talking to the media, holding press conferences. This is how it will be. He is not going to sit up on a mountainside hidden away. He is going to be at the forefront of our life from now on.

This is a fantastic opportunity for personal evolution. It is not that you will get it because you have done something so you deserve something back. A lot of people have that feeling about their service activity. They do not do it because they really want to serve. What they do is a bit of a bore but they do it because they think it is good for karma. They are chipping away at the big, heavy block of karma on their back all the time, and they think that everything they do is going to make a difference to the weight. If it is really service it would, but if it is compulsory, conditioned service then I doubt if it does. That is why some people do not change after years and years of what they call service, years and years of what they call meditation. They do not seem to change at all because their approach to it is not real. Their soul is not involved, and that is the problem.

False Personas

What do you mean by 'false personas'?

If you are determined that no one is ever going to 'put you down', that you are not going to be 'walked over', used, manipulated, or made less than in fact you think you are — if you take up such a defensive attitude to every situation and get 'hard' and aggressive — that is a persona you have adopted. It is not you.

Most people who know their ray structure put their personality down to the expression of their rays. It is often nothing to do with rays. If you could see their parents, you would see why they are like that. If it is a woman, you would say: "I know what the mother was like." They are simply taking up a position for or against their mother. They project into every situation that persona of aggression and defensiveness, keeping themselves intact and giving nothing, not allowing anyone to 'walk over them', as they see it.

That is a false persona. It is not what the person is like. It is not what intuitively their response as a soul would be, and it gets in the way. You know in your own group the people that you can talk to reasonably, whose mind is open, who are thoughtful about themselves, who will quickly try to change if it is pointed out to them or it becomes obvious that they are thought to be too bossy, obstreperous, 'pushy' or whatever.

If they are thoughtful, they will usually make some effort to change. Unless people do this, they maintain a false persona, which might be of recent construction. I was talking about the old persona, the persona we bring out of our school life and maintain in a completely false way. Many people are made up entirely of false personalities, sometimes several. They adopt them in any given circumstance to present the right kind of face — one they expect to be taken seriously, accepted as nice, amenable, diplomatic, thoughtful or kind, whether they are like that or not.

People go through life from childhood, through their school life, and are impacted by their peers on everything that they think and do. They have to be on a level with them, better if possible, but if not better at least level, acceptably the same. In the USA that desire for acceptability is rather pronounced at any level. There is competition, but also competition to be accepted. That means being the same as everyone else — standing out, but not being different, being forceful but not being forceful in a different way — so that everyone is acceptable.

These are false personas people adopt in order to fit in, to be liked, to be taken seriously, in order not to be bullied. These are different psychological facsimiles of possible selves that people construct in order to fit into life. They bring all of this into the group situation. With those who help them to achieve that condition, where they feel satisfied, accepted, at ease, they do their very best to maintain that situation.

Few rethink their personality. Few consider whether what they say to other people is actually the truth, or whether it was something they heard from someone else that made them laugh, and made them admire the person who said it. So they adopt it to be admired. Everyone imitates other people. We all imitate people whom we admire, whom we think will give us a better expression, however remote it might be from our own personality.

If it is in the so-called spiritual groups, that takes a very definite form. If it is in the 'New Age' groups, then you must, to quite a large extent, be able to roll your eyes upward and hold them there for long enough for people to recognize your spirituality and lack of materialistic focus. When money is being given out, you will be the first there but you should give the impression that money is of no concern to you at all: "I will borrow your money any time. Money is just energy, 3rd-ray energy, concretized — we all know that. Therefore, I can borrow any amount of your money without having to repay it. For myself, I do not have money because money is usually dirty. It is just tainted energy. That is why I do not actually do any job that would require my putting in hours in order to earn money because I am above that. I have reached a stage in my

107

evolutionary journey in which I am very conscious that money is not an end in itself. It is useful, at least other people's money is, if they will let me borrow it." I exaggerate, of course, to make the point.

These are personas which people present. I have met them by the thousands in this work. They are always giving me books about how nice we have to be to each other, how if there was only love and light in the world everything would be all right. That is one of the major glamours of the New Age groups: "If people only understood what I understand, that love and light are the very basis of life, the world would change. There would be no problems like Kosovo, Bosnia, or Northern Ireland." These so-called New Age/spiritual groups have the biggest glamours of all, and that is one of the main ones. They are not real, and therefore they do not know what real working relationships with other people are about because they have never worked in this way.

This is the essence of the 'New Age' background from which most people are drawn into the groups. If that is the background, it is no wonder that they cannot have impersonal group relationships. They always love some people and totally dislike the people who are like themselves, who have the same glamours. We always dislike our own glamours when we see them in other people. In ourselves we can stand them perfectly well but in other people they are hateful.

If they are in a business situation, working for a company, the same conditions will apply. They will get to know some members of the staff, come close to some, a little less close to others, and never talk to others. This same attitude is brought into the service activity where it is out of place. It is natural that because of rays, background, and interests, you will gravitate to the company of some people more than others. That is inevitable. But in terms of *consciousness*, there should not be other than impersonal group relations. Being in a service group requires the relationships between people to be impersonal. Unless you do that, you have not taken the very first step towards implementing the requirements for group initiation.

"Wearing of a Hood"

In the book Glamour — A World Problem *by the Master Djwhal Khul He quotes the 'Rules of the Road' for Disciples from the ancient archives. The injunctions are very beautiful and written in symbolic terms. Most are easily understandable (I think!) but one rule is rather abstruse: could you explain it please? "Rule 4: Three things the Pilgrim must avoid. The wearing of a hood, the veil which hides his face from others; the carrying of a water pot which only holds enough for his own wants; the shouldering of a staff without a crook to hold." It was particularly the last phrase which was difficult to interpret. Can you help please?* (July/August 2000)

(1) "The wearing of a hood ..." Many mystically-inclined disciples are so conscious of being 'different' and 'special' that they lose sight of themselves as ordinary members of society. They often adopt a spurious persona to hide their 'real' identity as disciples. Or, on the other hand, they may lack the courage to 'stand up and be counted' for what they believe and are.

(2) "The carrying of a water pot ..." This refers to the need for sharing, not only of the material things of life, but of that which has been accrued in terms of knowledge and understanding on the Path.

(3) "The shouldering of a staff without a crook to hold." This refers to the necessity for the disciples to have a firm basis on which to proceed. A disciple means one who is disciplined, serious, constant, one who stands firm in the midst of troubles, and whose "staff" is not easily knocked from his hand.

In the same book, Glamour — A World Problem, *the Master Djwhal Khul describes a glamour which He calls the Glamour of authority: at one point He describes the state in which one becomes imprisoned by one's love of independence or freedom. Later He gives as a solution to this problem the realization that the disciple walks not alone but that he lives and works in group relation and in obedience to group life. (1) Does this, and other glamours like the glamour of sentimentality and the glamour of materiality, still apply to groups working now — like those working for the Emergence? (2) Are these serious glamours?* (July/August 2000)

(1) Yes, indeed, very much so. (2) Yes, of course, they are very serious glamours which make the creation of correct group relationships so difficult. The idea and experience of group relationship is so new to most aspirants today that they find it hard to abandon — even to a small extent — their beloved 'independence' and 'freedom' which they see as their personality goal. No real progress can be made, however, until the soul impulse to unity and fusion makes itself felt and allows a correct relation to the group.

Overcoming of Glamour

What can we do daily to overcome glamour?

Look at the glamours, become self-aware, self-observant and, without condemning, recognize the glamours for what they are. Recognize how unreal they are. If we think about a glamour and look at it without condemning it, without trying to change it, we become more aware of its true nature. I think you will find in almost every case that it is different from what you thought because of the very nature of glamour. Glamour hides the truth, the reality. That being the case, it will be very different from the reality. This is why the Master Djwhal Khul could mistake His devotion to His Master for His highest quality, whereas it was actually the quality which was holding Him back. It is always so different from what you think. This is the difficulty in recognizing glamour.

We must not have sentimental relationships, etc, even though we have all these emotions. Should we suppress them, and act 'as if' we are mentally polarized? (January/February 1999)

We could put it this way: should you behave — not act — as if you are mentally polarized when you are still only 1.35, in the middle of the throes of astral polarization? The answer, then, is yes. If you do not behave as if you are mentally polarized, you will probably never become mentally polarized. But what does it mean? It does not mean to go around with a long face, looking wise. It means to act by throwing the light of the soul, through the mind, on what you do. That releases you from glamour. The value of mental polarization is that it frees you from the worst aspects of glamour by being able, through the mental body, to shine the light of the soul onto the glamour.

The problem of glamour is that it is a fog. You cannot see in a fog. While you are in the glamour, you cannot see it. When you see it, you can take steps to dissipate it. Being mentally polarized allows you increasingly to see and so remove the glamour. You can only do that if you *behave* — not act — as if you are already mentally polarized. If you go on indulging the glamours, even if you are beginning to be mentally polarized, you will still be glamoured. It does not happen from one day to the next — one moment you are 1.5, the next you are 1.6 and mentally polarized. That is only *the beginning* of the process of mental polarization. You still have to dissipate the fogs of glamour that go right up to 2.5, where spiritual polarization begins, and the soul is steadily pouring its light into the life of the disciple.

While you want to be who you are, you realize that you have been full of spiritual ambition. You recognize that as a glamour. You do not want that any more, but you want to be just who you are. You want to have your aspiration as well. (July 1998)

There is no point in being happy with, or accepting, illusion. Otherwise, you will never get out of the illusion. However, I do not think you should beat yourself with a whip and say: "I must get good. I must, I must, I must get good." People, literally, do that; they have done it for centuries.

We have to recognize what change means. Nobody changes overnight, dramatically and totally. They might change their habits but not their Being. If you know you are an immortal spiritual Being, then there is time for change. You have to have a long view, a sense of proportion. You have to have a reasonable sense of rhythm and forward movement but not the feeling of frenetic haste which is the desire principle at work, a big glamour. If you do not care too much you are more likely to make progress than if you care like billy-oh, and cannot wait a moment to become 'advanced'. It all depends on the focus: is it on the self or the world outside the self?

If you do this work, the aim should be to be as impersonal, as objective, as possible. Then in a sense it does not matter what your state of Being is, because it will right itself. If you work objectively in preparing for the externalization of the Hierarchy, for example, educating the public in the laws of life and the constitution of humanity, very subtly and gradually you will change, without your even trying or noticing. Your glamours will fall away if you do not think too much about them, and do not go around hating yourself for having them. Forget *yourself.* We have glamours because we are at the centre of the universe. If we can stop being the centre, and instead become objective and impersonal — by 'impersonal' meaning to put ourselves out of the picture — the glamours will fall away. As long as we are

112

holding on to the picture of being good or bad, ourself or not ourself, we will be filled with the glamour of the self.

The lower self is the cause of all the problems. As soon as we can act impersonally, we cannot help but grow. Then the soul smiles a big, radiant smile because we are doing what the soul is trying to do: bend to its will this recalcitrant, rebellious, individual who keeps pushing himself or herself to the centre of the world. We are not the centre of the world — we cannot all be at the centre. We have to recognize that we are a god but only one god among many, and none of us in this one incarnation is all that important. This sense of importance, even the importance of development, of advancing and becoming a great server and getting rid of our glamour — even that is a glamour. It all comes from the sense of the self as being separate.

My advice is to put that aside and just do the work. Forget everything else but the work. Forget about the internecine strife that goes on in every group, more or less. Just do the work — coolly and calmly. The idea that seems to me to simplify the whole thing is to put yourself out of the way. Where glamour is concerned, the less you think about yourself the less glamoured you are showing yourself to be.

Glamour is the sense of the separated self. It is the great illusion. As the astral light (the light of the astral planes) pours down into the world, more and more of this illusion will be dissipated. But if you are grappling with the problem of glamour, as everyone is, consciously or unconsciously, the question is: how do we do it? The first step, it seems to me, is to become impersonal. That does not mean cold or 'scientific', although it is a scientific approach to life. It is the way of the Buddha and the Christ. It is the way of every great teacher who has ever achieved anything. You have to put yourself out of the picture and simply serve. Why? Because it has to be done, because the world is there to be served. Why do people climb

Mount Everest? Because it is there. Why do people serve the world? Because of the pain and suffering, the lack of light, the lack of knowledge in the world. Fulfil that and you will make your own life so much happier.

I understand it is glamour that prevents me from acting when I identify with my emotions and thoughts. I feel joy when I move my focus from the personal to the group. We can overcome glamour by seeing the situation through mind. Are these the same? If different, what is different? (Japanese Conference (JC) May 2000)

The illusion of every level, physical, emotional, or mental, is overcome by the activity of the level above it. So the illusion of the physical plane, which is called *maya*, is overcome by the aspirational quality of the emotional body. When the aspiration is high enough it achieves a control of the activity of the physical elemental.

The illusion of the astral plane, what we call glamour, is overcome by soul light focused on it from the mental plane.

Illusion of the mental plane is called, simply, illusion. It is dispersed by the light of the soul, which we call intuition. By right use of the intuition, the illusionary aspect of the mental plane is overcome.

Another name for intuition, which destroys illusion, is *buddhi*. It comes from the *buddhic* level of the spiritual triad of the soul. The function that *buddhi* has on the mental plane is to end the sense of separation. Illusion of every kind, physical, emotional, and mental, is the result of the basic fault in our consciousness that we are separate when we are not. That is the beginning of glamour. As soon as you sense that you are separate, glamour begins. You can see how endemic in the race glamour is, because that is our major fault in seeing reality. We experience ourselves as dual. There is us and there is that 'out there'. Yet we are one and the same. There is no separation. There is no duality. As long as we experience the duality, we experience glamour of some kind at some level.

There is an entity borne out of our constant personality experiences. As the soul incarnates, it creates a personality. The sum total of all the personality experiences, over aeons of time, is given the name of 'The Dweller on the Threshold'. Through various lives one deals with the illusion of the physical plane, *maya*, then the glamour of the astral plane, and then the illusions of the mental plane. Eventually, the Dweller on the Threshold, the sum total of all of these glamours, or unrealities, or sense of dualism, meets the soul, the 'Angel of the Presence' as it is called, and confronts its true reality. One day all that glamour is dissipated and the person is free at last of illusion.

Is it possible for me to prevent myself from mistaking other people's opinions for my own and conditioning myself to be such and such? (JC May 2000)

Yes, it is possible. Anything is possible. It may be difficult for some people and easier for others. There are some people who never bend to other people's opinions, who are so sure of their being right that it is not a problem. For the person asking the question, of course, it is. It is a common one, a fight between the soul and the personality. Some personalities, given certain rays, may be rather unsure of themselves and very readily take other people's opinions and ways of thinking, and use them as an example of how to act. Because of their aspiration, which basically is a soul quality coming originally from the soul through the astral body, they try to do the best thing. They are stirred by the idea of a cause. There is nothing wrong in this.

It is a question of finding the balance between one's own self and one's own life, and the sense of reality, common sense, and the inspiration of serving a cause. It is a question of establishing a rhythm which you can intelligently and actively sustain.

What is the best attitude to have to the Reappearance work?

Some people are stirred for a little while, do tremendous work and then they do nothing for months. In all the groups around the world there are people who suddenly start attending the group meetings just two or three weeks before I am due to come. They cannot do enough with the group. These are the people who really consider they are preparing the way for Maitreya. They are not. They are doing something to make themselves feel satisfied and at ease. A steady rhythm is accepting the work that has to be done and doing it because it has to be done, doing it impersonally, objectively. This is the best way to proceed and a way you can keep up indefinitely.

The work of these groups, whose task it is to make the initial approach to the public, is stated by the Master Djwhal Khul, through Alice Bailey, to be the most difficult job of all, except for the political groups. There are many people who like doing work, even in group formation, for a short time, while it is jolly and interesting and new. When it gets difficult, when they have to work for a long time, over years and years, then this is the work that, as we say in English, "sorts out the men from the boys".

You say tolerance is a necessity. But if you do not have tolerance how can you be tolerant? Am I to direct back to myself what I see in others, regardless of what I see, thinking they are all my glamours?

They may not be your glamours. You have to be as objective as possible. If you do not have tolerance, you have to get tolerance. If you do not have money, you have to earn or borrow some money, get it somehow. If it is money, you will get it. If it is tolerance you need, you may or may not get it. It is up to you. No one else can give you tolerance. It is something which has to come out of yourself, a vision of the world. If you see something lacking in yourself, you have to try to build it in. That means self-observation. Without condemning yourself, you should be aware of your motives. Are you as pure, righteous, tolerant, giving and just, as you would like other people to be?

I would like to have your interpretation of the usefulness of common sense in relation to overcoming glamours. (JC May 2000)

Common sense is not only useful in relation to overcoming glamours, it is absolutely essential. Unfortunately, so-called common sense is the least common sense that exists. One could almost say that of all the qualities absent in most aspirants and disciples in relation to life generally, and therefore to their glamours, the most frequently absent is precisely a lack of common sense. This is particularly true in relation to certain rays like the 2nd ray and probably, above all, the 6th ray. Of all the rays, the 6th ray seems to be the most lacking in common sense, because it is always focused on the astral plane and reflects all its hopes, desires and ideals onto every event it experiences. It senses itself as the centre of the universe, its only reality is everything *it* feels, hopes, thinks, and aspires toward. Therefore, it has no common sense.

The use of the words 'New Age type' refers particularly to the type we are discussing who believes that everything he feels, hopes, is devoted to, is the only reality, when most of it is unreal. It is simply aspiration. This is the one who is usually the thorn in the flesh of every group, who is always right while all the other members of the group are always wrong. They do not have the common sense to say: "Is it likely, given the nature of life, that I will always be right and they will always be wrong? Is

117

it feasible?" The answer, of course, is 'no', but they never come to that answer because they never ask the question.

What is common sense? Obviously it is not common. It is very uncommon, especially in New Age groups. Common sense is more the innate intelligence of the race of human beings enhanced and refined by the quality of the soul, in so far as that can play on the *manasic* or intelligence factor. It is not exactly intuition, but shares some of its qualities with what is the true soul quality of intuition. It is a kind of intelligent awareness that gives, above all, a sense of proportion. That is not only useful but absolutely essential in overcoming glamours.

(1) What characteristics most hinder disciples? (2) What characteristics are considered most positive in discipleship? (June 2000)

(1) Fear, inertia, self-interest, attachment, ambition. (2) Courage, detachment, steadfastness, sense of proportion, aspiration.

If, as a disciple, I know that I have certain neurotic tendencies which I have difficulty in controlling, should I talk about my problems with others in the group? Or should I just try and forget about them? (June 2000)

If talking helps, then why not talk? Consider these tendencies as glamours and deal with them in that light.

Will the outpouring of Maitreya's love on Declaration Day sublimate our glamours (samsaras) and illusions and allow us consciously to evolve? (July/August 1997)

Not all and not totally, by any means, but it will go a long way towards it.

Courage and Detachment

How does lack of courage keep us glamoured? Is courage important to the vitality of the group?

Courage is absolutely essential to any disciple. If you are not courageous, you will never become a Master. We have to learn to live alone *in consciousness*, in order to become a Master. To be bereft of all guidance, all higher direction, to be absolutely alone *in consciousness* in the world, which is what you feel when you become a fourth-degree initiate because you are bereft of the soul. Until that time the soul has been the highest aspect of which you could be aware. As you advance, you become more and more aware of being the soul, but there comes a time at the fourth initiation in which that awareness ends. That is what Jesus was expressing when He said: "My God, my God, why have you forsaken me?" It is not a question of being forsaken by God. It is a question of: "Where have You gone? I thought I knew who God was, that is, my higher self, my soul, which is an exact reflection of God. What has happened?" It is no longer there, because it has been absorbed again into the Self, which is all deity, the Divine itself.

After the fourth initiation you are alone in a way that no one in this room has ever been alone. That takes courage. The Master is absolutely alone, although one of a Brotherhood. You have to be able to be totally alone to be a Master, and that means you have to develop courage. The way to develop it is to show courage in every situation; face the situation, and grow in courage. If you grow in courage in the little things, it makes courage easier in the big things, like being alone in the whole of cosmos. It is a frightening thought unless you have courage. So not to have courage keeps you glamoured in the sense that you will never grow.

Glamour is the result of the kind of consciousness that does not change. The very nature of life is change; it is essential. There is nothing more real in the whole of cosmos than change. Change happens and you have no control over it except in very minor ways in your own mind. The change that takes place as life finds new forms, new modes of expression, is outside your control.

The first fish that came out of the sea and took up living on dry land experienced a change which it never contemplated. There is a mechanism we call aspiration, which from its very nature drove the fish out of the sea onto the land. It aspired to a different condition. The nature of desire is glamour, but at the same time it is in every single rock and stone, in matter itself. There is no such thing as dead matter; all matter is conscious. It is the consciousness of the atom, the desire principle inherent in every atom in the universe, that drove the fish out of the sea and onto dry land, to become a mammal and eventually a human being.

That process is envisioned by the Logos, not just as a physical possibility; it is envisioned first of all, as everything is, in energetic terms. The energies make it inevitable. So the change takes place from sea creature to land creature from the principle of desire itself, aspiration, the very nature of life. It takes courage to do that. Not all fish did it at first. They would go up to the edge and say: "Oh no, not me. It is not wet out there. How am I going to survive?" But then some fish came along, probably a 4th-ray type, who said: "It is dry out there. Okay, here I go, follow me!" Like the Hussar attacking the guns with his sword, saying: "Follow me!" Is courage important to the vitality of the group? Of course. Courage is probably what is lacking in most groups. It takes courage to speak publicly to sceptics about the Reappearance, to your friends and family even. It takes courage to swim against the tide of public opinion, to talk openly about such a controversial subject. That is why so many people prefer to spend their time on the internet. It is easier, by far.

Are experiences of aloneness in the earlier stages of the initiatory path indicative of that which is to come as one progresses? (January/February 1999)

Yes, to some extent. At some time or other in our life's progress we have to learn to stand alone. Aloneness, in the sense that I mean it, is being detached. We have to reach a point where what happens to us is not all that important; what other people think about us, not important at all; what other people say to us and however they vilify us, not important, easily overcome. We have to be able to take criticism and not criticize. If we were to put everything in one word, detachment is the key to the process of evolution.

Detachment is getting rid of the self. Attachment is seeing the self as at the centre of the world. Detachment is forgetting that there is a centre of the world and that it is us. Detachment is using the physical, astral, and mental equipment to express the soul, as far as we possibly can. How do we do that? Through creativity. Not by saying: "I am the soul, I am the soul! I must spread my soul light, my intuition, my knowledge, my wisdom!" That is glamour; we are still at the centre of the universe. Instead, we become impersonal. We hardly think about ourselves in that sense. We are not struggling with ourself to do this or do that. We are struggling with the work — to get it out, to make it known, to get work done in time for a deadline. It is the work, the reaching out, the meditation, the study, the growing awareness, the winding up of the spiritual clock, the spiritual spring.

That is only possible if we work in a detached way. Maitreya advocates honesty of mind, sincerity of spirit, and detachment. The greatest of these is detachment. We can only be truly honest in our mind if we are detached. We can only be sincere in our spirit when we are detached. Of course, we can only be detached when we are sincere in spirit and honest in mind. These three work together, but they arrive at detachment — detachment from wrong identification: never thinking that this body is the Self or that our emotions are true. Our emotions are never true. We think our emotions are not only real but that they are justified and the truest thing we could possibly feel at the time. No emotion is real; it is a dream. These fantasies are never true.

Emotion is a fantasy, a glamour of the astral planes, in which we are floating as in sleep. We think that our emotions are true and real, and that this body is real. If you could see your body from the angle of the soul, you would see it as transparent, like an image on a cinema screen. All of physical-plane life is a cinema screen, and we know how real is the cinema screen. While we are entranced, we take it to be real. Essentially, it is a flat screen with images of 'life' thrown on it; it is not real. Least real of all are our emotions, our feelings — those precious feelings of anger, disappointment, self-pity and the rest.

(1) How can we start to become detached from our physical, astral and mental bodies? (2) Is it from the will of our own ego? (3) How can you become detached from the mind without using the mind itself? (June 1998)

It is not a question of becoming detached *from* these three bodies but rather of becoming detached from *identifying* with them as the Self. This makes for a growing awareness of who, indeed, we are.

What Prevents our Steps toward Group Initiation?

Rule Eleven

(1) The achieving of a non-sentimental group interrelation

(2) Learning how to use the forces of destruction constructively

(3) Attaining the power to work as a miniature Hierarchy, and as a group to exemplify unity in diversity

(4) Cultivating the potency of occult silence

(From: Alice A. Bailey, *The Rays and the Initiations*, Lucis Press, London, 1960)

It has been many years since you talked to us about the possibility of group initiation and instructed us to work toward it. Do you have any further insights on why we have not come closer to achieving group initiation?

The main reason is that it is difficult. It is the most difficult thing for any group in the world to achieve, which is why it has never been achieved. If it had been easy, groups would have achieved it many times before. For centuries the Masters have been attempting various experiments with groups, with the hope that one or other would achieve or come near to achieving group initiation, and that has never happened. Every experiment has failed. They have failed for a number of reasons, mainly to do with the glamours existing in all disciples.

One of the major reasons for this failure has been the absence of a powerful, magnetic idea that could hold together a group of individuals who do not know each other and are spread all over the world, as is this particular group. I talk about the Japanese, American, South African, European, Australian and New Zealand, etc, groups, but actually these are all members of one group. That group is working at the present time with the colossal, magnetic idea of the Reappearance of the Christ, the externalization of the work of the Spiritual Hierarchy. If that is not magnetic and powerful enough to hold these groups together, then nothing else would be. I cannot think of, and obviously the Masters have not been able to present, an idea which would be so powerful as to hold together groups with their own backgrounds and traditions, spread throughout the world, who may or may not have studied the Ageless Wisdom Teachings.

Why have we not come closer? Glamour is the reason for not being able, so far, even to begin to implement the process needed to bring about group initiation.

I was asked recently if we could go on and deal with a further aspect of the teaching of the requirements, Rule XII rather than Rule XI, because Rule XI has been, it was thought, well and truly studied, digested, and perhaps implemented. The Master said: "No group has *even begun* the process of implementing the four requirements of Rule XI." Until they are implemented, nothing towards group initiation can take place.

The hardest rule of all, it seems, the one that really engages people precisely at their glamours, is the requirement for impersonal group relationships. That seems to be a tough one for every group, because of the personality glamours of liking and disliking. The requirement for achieving impersonal group relationships is that they should not be based on liking or disliking. These are opposites, and you have to go beyond the pairs of opposites, however they express themselves. We like some people and can work with them, and we dislike others and cannot. These personality reactions have no place in occult groups.

Occult groups are not about personalities. They are the expression on the physical plane of a grouping of souls that are brought together through karmic law, ashramic necessity, and soul purpose or intention. That makes the occult group the kind that would take group initiation. We are not talking about a group of people forming a football team, or a group of businessmen forming a new company. That is a completely different thing. This is a group of souls working consciously on the soul level, coming into incarnation at the same time under ashramic necessity. The Masters know which disciples, at any given time, with certain ray structures, at a certain point in evolution, can, possibly, be stimulated and guided into a relationship that will make group initiation possible — that is to say, impersonal group relationships.

Most people cannot be impersonal. This is the crux of the whole thing. If you can be truly impersonal, you can do almost anything. Objectivity and impersonality are the hallmarks of the disciple who is ready for initiation. Most people demonstrate, even if they have taken the first initiation, that the nut of impersonality seems to be a very difficult one to crack.

If you don't like your fellow group members or the way they work and approach things but you want to work for the Emergence of Maitreya and the Masters, what should you do? (June 2000)

Try to get above the stage of liking and disliking, and try to see them as, like you, *souls* in incarnation doing their best for the same cause. In other words, try to be more tolerant, more detached, more impersonal in the group relationship. Look at yourself and ask yourself why you do not like the other members or their ways of working.

You said we have made little or no progress in the past two years in bringing more of the soul influence into our group work. When it comes to group initiation we not only have not taken Rule XI seriously, but some of us do not even understand Rule XI. Is this because, as the Master says in His message 'Unity', we are putting too great an emphasis on individuals and personality differences? (January/February 2002)

Yes, of course, what else? It is exactly that. Not other people's personality differences but your own, putting too great an emphasis on your own self, your own personality, your own different opinion, and not only on those of other people. Everybody is doing it, so that there is no real consensus; but also because fundamentally you cannot see the other members of the group in the right way.

What should motivate the group work as a whole, and which is essential to group unity, is an unspoken love between all the people in the group. But it is not "I love you, darling," every day. That is not right group relations. It is an unspoken, understood love that unites all the people. The real uniting factor is the work, to which everybody comes from themselves, from their soul level. The work is the thing. So that everything that they do, they do for the work as a co-worker. It is specifically the work that is the fundamental core of all the activity of the group. It is not to do with making nice relationships with other members, getting on well with others, not speaking in too loud a voice, not making your own ideas known too often. It is about the work, putting forward the work and *forgetting yourself.* If people would forget themselves, they would have right human relations. It is simple because then they are working as souls, and since the soul only knows about right human relationships it becomes instinctive.

They will work in relation to their co-workers as souls and automatically make the right kind of relationship which moves

126

towards the implementation of Rule XI. People think they must not have personal relations. It must not be *built* on personal relations. It does not mean that you are not to have personal relations, but what you do has to be built around the work and not around personal relations. People do not understand this and so they go on in the old way, thinking: "Do I like this person?" or: "I cannot work with this person."

There will be people in the group with whom you do not want to work. You do not like the personality. Perhaps it is the ray you do not like, or the way they were brought up. There are many reasons why you might like or not like, but that is not the level on which you should work. You work with people because of the work, which is for the reappearance of the Christ. That colours the quality of what you do. Therefore you have to work with people with whom, ordinarily, you would never work.

It is not to do with the personality needs or habits, but with the recognition of another person's soul's response to this tremendous idea. There is no bigger idea in the whole of the world. What is happening now is the most important event in 98,000 years. The Christ is *in the world*, not just someone you read about in a book. It is the return to the world of the Christ, plus Jesus, plus the other Masters, out on the physical plane as a group for the first time for 98,000 years.

Is it possible to move towards group initiation without group unity? (January/February 2002)

No, it is absolutely impossible. If you do not have group unity, you do not have the qualities in the group that you need to have group initiation. You have to study Rule XI. In Rule XI there are four major requirements that each member of the group has to be able to demonstrate in group formation. Unless they can do that, not only do they not have group unity, they are, as yet, far from group initiation.

In the rules for group initiation, there is the rule about using the forces of destruction constructively. I did not understand that at all. (January/February 2002)

Using the forces of destruction in a constructive way is using them to destroy the glamours that prevent right relations. We have discussed how destructive criticism is to the unity of a group. If the members of a group go around criticizing each other, as they do from time to time in some groups, there cannot be right relationships. There are groups which seem not to desire unity at all, in which the desire for unity seems to be missing.

You cannot have unity if there is no desire for it. That is why the Master says very clearly, the first thing is that you have to desire unity. You have to see it as a treasure that gives a tremendous richness to the life of the group because it relates to the fundamental nature of our life, all life, because we are part of the One Life. There are some individuals who, because of their ray structure, point in evolution, upbringing, a combination of reasons, are always criticizing, always breaking up the unity of a group. They must be different and are therefore destructive.

Whereas the others want just to get on with filling the envelopes or doing the designs for a poster. It is always people who do not do anything who are the destructive ones. They use the conflict in their own nature to upset the spontaneous unity which exists when a group of people who all believe in the same cause are working happily in promoting it and are doing it in a completely unified and uncomplicated way.

People have to learn, and they find it very hard. That is why these rules are given. Without them being part of your nature, instinctive in the working of the group, the group never comes to group initiation. This is the truth, I am afraid. It is very hard. People do not seem to understand them. If they understand the words, they do not understand the need for them.

What is the balance between having a group leader, as in a mini-hierarchy, and having full group participation?

It is not a question of balance. They are different things. You should not see the ability to act as a mini-hierarchy as requiring hierarchical differences in the group. What the Master Djwhal Khul is talking about is that automatically, in any group, there will be people at different levels. Perhaps someone is around 0.95, and several who have just taken the first initiation, 1.0 up to 1.2, for example. There will be those a bit more advanced who are 1.3 to 1.5. Then there might be one or two between 1.5 and 1.7. Rarely, there might be someone above 1.7.

What the Master Djwhal Khul means is that there should be someone in every group who is in *conscious* relation to Hierarchy; that is the ideal. I perform that task in this group — taking this group to mean all the people in all our groups around the world. There needs to be people who can take the requirements from Hierarchy as interpreted by me and implement them as far as possible in the world: produce books, magazines and literature of all kinds; hold meetings, contact media, act as the liaison between me and the world.

I am doing that plus my own work — the contact with the Masters and the actual, practical, dissemination of the information. Then there are those who do only Transmission Meditation. They are not too involved in the day-to-day work but often they will put up posters and that kind of work. The giving of your time and energy is service. The group automatically falls into this mini-hierarchical situation, but it should be conscious.

It is not a question of balance between having a group leader in a mini-hierarchy and having full group participation. There should *always* be the latter. I am working in London on a day-to-day basis, and I do not think the people in London have any sense of not participating.

In all aspects of group work is it my glamour, namely fear, which causes me to suppress my own opinion when I hear so-and-so saying otherwise? I see myself telling myself that I must work in a mini-hierarchy, meaning that person may be higher and, therefore, I should suppress my own ideas and listen to them instead. (JC May 2000)

Yes, this is certainly glamour. In particular I would say the glamour of the 2nd ray where the natural timidity and fear of the 2nd-ray personality (not soul) is in this case rationalizing that fear by making an excuse for it in accepting the idea of a mini-hierarchy and, therefore, bowing to the ideas of others.

The Masters form a hierarchy according to Their various grades. So, naturally, a Master of the fifth degree would take the advice, the awareness, the decisions of the Christ, Maitreya, as a matter of course because He is a seventh-degree initiate and would know things that the fifth-degree initiate, even though He is a Master, could not possibly know. But the Masters also work as a democracy. Every Master has the right to make His voice heard on whatever subject, but, of course, He will only do so if He believes that He has something of importance to add. It is not simply the passing of an opinion. In our groups there is nobody so much higher than another that they should bow to the thoughts of somebody they think is higher. The differences in evolution in the different groups is minimal.

To work as a mini-hierarchy does not mean paying undue respect to the ideas of others. It means working at your level. It means if you are 1.3 or 1.5 you work at that level. You do not pretend to be working at 3.5, which means sitting back and watching the others do the work and directing them. I know groups in which people who have not yet taken the second initiation act as if they were sixth-degree initiates.

Even if you are 1.2, could you be expressing 1.0 consciousness?
(JC May 2000)

It is not possible to be higher or lower than your given level. The level is designated by the area of consciousness, the polarization. Up until 1.5 to 1.6 the polarization is on the astral plane. That means it is impossible to be other than astrally polarized while at that level. However, almost everybody advances in an irregular manner, not with all aspects going forward at the same rate. So somebody might be very advanced along a certain point of his or her being and less so in another. For example, the third-degree initiate has control of the physical, the astral and the mental vehicles. The vibrational rate of all three bodies is synchronous; vibrating together at the same rate. However, you only have to look at the life history of some third-degree initiates to find that it may be quite unequal. It will depend on their rays and their ability to synthesize these on the various levels. That person is a living soul but from an average point of view, may do deeds which are not at a level that you would expect at his point of evolution.

For example, Adolph Hitler was not a very nice person. In fact, he was a real horror, but he was already a second-degree initiate. From the point of view of a soul he was perfect. From the point of view of the man, even as a second-degree initiate he was probably one of the most dangerous personalities that we have as yet created.

Each man is a lighthouse and sheds abroad his light for his brother. Make bright your lamp and let it shine forth and show the way.

All are needed, every one.
No one is too small or young to take part in this Great Plan for the rescue and the rehabilitation of our world.

Resolve to do this and be assured that My help will not be withheld.

From Message No. 13 – 19 January 1978

Implementing the Requirements for Group Initiation

How much should the groups focus directly on studying the requirements for group initiation, or will progress towards group initiation happen naturally as we work co-operatively on the Reappearance?

To some degree, yes, if the attitude of the group is correct. However, we can imagine that we are working co-operatively for the Reappearance and not make the slightest progress towards group initiation. It is not so much studying but implementing the requirements. That is exactly what the Master said. No group has even begun to implement the requirements. The major obstacle is the lack of impersonal relationships. People are not able to be impersonal.

If you are working truly co-operatively, you probably are working in the right relationship, but it does not just happen naturally. Nothing really happens by itself. It is as Maitreya says: "Man must act and implement his will." If you want something to happen you have to implement it; you have to act to bring it about.

This is one of the problems for many 6th-ray people. They tend to imagine that if they can visualize something, put a name on it, it is already there. But it is not real. It is a dream, an astral vision only. It is a possibility but until you actually put it into effect and make it real on the physical plane, it does not exist as other than a dream. Americans call their life a dream. "Act out your dreams." This phrase is presented to Americans to "live your dream", but what do you mean by "dream"? It would be different for different people — a comfortable life, a fruitful marriage with lots of children, a good school for them so that they grow up and get a good job. It is all very contrived.

I am talking about the ability of powerfully 6th-ray-influenced people to visualize, actually to envision an ideal. That ideal might be terrible for some, but they envision it as the ideal. You envision the best of all possible lives — peace, prosperity, and abundance for everyone, black and white. You present this to everyone as your idea of life, but until you begin to implement it, it does not exist. It is only an astral dream, imagination, an idealistic idea. That is the problem, and I find it as much in the groups as in the nation as a whole.

Of course it is not just in the United States. I find the same thing wherever that ray is powerfully at work in the groups — the idea that if you can name a thing, envision it, idealize it, then, without making it form, without structuring it on the physical plane, you get the feeling that it is done. But it has not been done at all. It is just like a dream, you wake up and it is not there. When Americans wake up, they will see that freedom and justice do not live in America, at least not for everyone. They do for white people on the whole, but not for the 30 million who live below the poverty line, and certainly they are not present for black people on the whole, and certainly not for the world as a whole. It is just a dream, an idea.

If you are working co-operatively you will probably be doing the right kind of activity vis-à-vis the Reappearance, but that is not the same as working in a group in an impersonal manner above and beyond likes and dislikes. Impersonality is an attitude in which liking and not liking do not enter into the picture. That is why impersonality is so rare. There are other factors, but that is the first, and, it would appear, the most difficult factor in creating right human relations.

What is the relationship between group initiation and the Reappearance work? What is more important? Is it enough to

*focus on the Reappearance work and leave the group initiation
as a by-product?*

It is not 'either/or'. If you are correctly conducting the work of
the Reappearance *as a group*, you will be addressing the
requirements for group initiation. The question is how you do it.
Do you really do it in the ways laid down in the four rules of
Rule XI? Do you really have impersonal group relationships?
Do you really work as a mini-hierarchy? Do you really observe
the law of occult silence? Do you really use the forces of
destruction in a constructive way? If the answer to any of these
questions is no, then that is what you have to do. Otherwise, you
are playing with the idea of group initiation.

You have to work at the Reappearance work by behaving as
if you are this mini-hierarchy, behaving with impersonal group
relationships, observing occult silence, and using the forces of
destruction in a constructive way. That is how it is done. It is not
either/or. One, as it is carried out, should involve the action of
the other.

*(1) While it is said that the progress of one member of a group
benefits all in the group can this also be seen in reverse? (2) Is
it also possible that the failings and weaknesses of one or some
members can serve as a brake on the rest of the group? (3) Is it
true, in other words, that a group is as strong as its weakest
link?* (June 2000)

(1) Yes. (2) Yes. (3) That does not necessarily follow.

*(1) If some groups are more successful from a Hierarchical
point of view does that mean that each member puts more soul
'effort' into all the activities involved? (2) Can it also be that,
while some members are less evolved, others balance that by
allowing more of their soul input or more intuition to
demonstrate in the group work?* (June 2000)

(1) Yes. (2) Yes, precisely.

Has there been any improvement at all in the soul-personality balance given for the various groups since your keynote talk on Glamour in 1999? Many groups have really improved their activities and many more people are very busy and do much more outreach work than ever before; has that changed the balance now? (June 2000)

No. It is not really a question of how busy or hardworking a group is or attempts to be. It is a question of the relation between the soul input of the group and that stemming from the separative personality. Where the soul input is high the work will be of high quality and, of course, vice versa.

What should the correct attitude be to service? Some of us seem to work out of habit and routine (and sometimes apparently without any joy), others out of an idealistic aspiration which sometimes sweeps us along into activities which might not be thoroughly thought out, others seem to work in fits and starts and when it suits us, while there are others who seem to be finding some kind of personality fulfilment in the work. (June 2000)

In most groups at this (early) stage of group activity, some or all of these attitudes can be found. The ideal attitude is one of sustained, impersonal dedication to the group cause carried out with joy — and, preferably, humour and tolerance.

[For more information on group initiation, see Benjamin Creme, *Maitreya's Mission, Volume Two*, Chapter 19 'Toward Group Initiation']

My dear friends, I am happy indeed to be among you once more in this fashion, and to set before you some guidelines for the future.

My task will be to show you how to live together peacefully as brothers. This is simpler than you imagine, My friends, for it requires only the acceptance of Sharing. Sharing, indeed, is divine. It underlies all progress for man.
By its means, My brothers and sisters, you can come into correct relationship with God; and this, My friends, underlies your lives.
When you share, you recognize God in your brother.
This is a Truth, simple, but until now difficult for man to grasp.
The time has come to evidence this Truth.

By My Presence the Law of Sharing will become manifest.
By My Presence man will grow to God.
By the Presence of Myself and My Brothers, the New Country of Love shall be known.
Take, My friends, this simple Law to your hearts.
Manifest Love through Sharing, and change the world.
Create around you the atmosphere of Peace and Joy, and with Me make all things new.

My Coming portends change; likewise, grief at the loss of the old structures.
But, My friends, the old bottles must be broken — the new wine deserves better.
My friends, My brothers, I am near you now.
I see above and around you your aspiration for Love and Joy.
I know this to be widespread in mankind; this makes possible My Return.

Let Me unveil for you your divine inheritance.
Let Me show you the wonders of God which yet await you.
Allow Me to take you simply by the hand and lead you to the Forest of Love, the Glade of Peace, the River of Truth.

Take My hand, My friends, and know this to be yours, now.

Message No. 82 – 12 September 1979

EXPLOSION OF GLAMOUR

[The following is an edited version of the keynote talk given by Benjamin Creme in May 1999 at the Transmission Meditation Conference in Shiga, Japan.]

You can never work too much, too often, too continuously, on glamour. As the day of Maitreya's emergence comes closer, I have found a sudden explosion of glamour in the different groups, not just here in Japan but all over the world.

Glamours that seem to have been subdued, controlled, overcome for years, have suddenly flowered in a renaissance of glamour. It seems that the more powerful the energies of Maitreya become in the world — the energy of equilibrium, the energies of Aquarius — the more this excites and activates the glamours in the groups. You can see this in the outer world as well: sudden explosions of war in different areas; extraordinary explosions, even among young children, who go into the schoolyard and shoot their colleagues; sudden eruptions of what is, fundamentally, human glamour. It is the astral-plane reaction to the incoming of the great spiritual energies of Maitreya. One would have hoped that the spiritual groups, especially those connected with the emergence of Hierarchy, would be in control of this situation, beyond this glamour, but it does not appear to be the case.

Maitreya has made Himself more available. He has made appearances in one guise or another to many members of the groups around the world, and this has excited their astral reaction. This works out in two ways: the over-excitation of those immediately involved in the appearances, which is perhaps only to be expected, and fundamentally not too harmful; much more harmful is the response of other members to the experiences of those who have had some kind of contact with Maitreya. Instead of pleasure at the good fortune of the individuals concerned there have often been powerful reactions of jealousy, which are bad for the individuals who experience them and for the group as a whole.

There is a general, excited, astral reaction to the sense that the time is growing near for Maitreya's appearance. Some very over-excited reactions are taking place around the world. Maitreya does not really come to give us excitement. He comes to teach us the art of living. Although excitement is to be expected, it also has to be controlled, and channelled along useful lines. This requires honesty with oneself and with the group about the nature of our reactions. When you realize you have responded to events in terms of glamour, it is no good putting it aside and saying: "Well, I did not really feel that." You will only change and grow when you admit openly to yourself and others that indeed your response was glamour, was spiteful, jealous or hateful. You cannot pretend to yourself or to the group, because it will always work inside you until you tell the truth. Only then can you have correct group relations. That is the ideal, of course, and the ideal is seldom achieved, certainly not today, but the group should *aim* towards that kind of honesty.

It behoves spiritual groups to work in a different way from 'ordinary' human beings or groups. A spiritual person, and therefore a spiritual group, is someone who has accepted the spiritual dimension of themselves, that they are souls in incarnation. Therefore, the group relationships should be of a different kind from ordinary, everyday human relationships as they are today.

The average human being's relationships to other people is based largely on their personality, and therefore on glamour.

Since the vast majority of humanity is astrally polarized, this is inevitable. An aspirant or disciple is seeking to raise the polarization point higher and higher. Having become aware of the soul, their spiritual identity, they should be, and ordinarily would be, seeking to polarize themselves at a spiritual level. The average human being who is not an aspirant spends much of his or her life in competition, in spiteful relationships, longstanding hatreds and resentments, in jealous reactions to other people's successes. Instead of sharing with pleasure in the successes of their friends and neighbours, they often have spiteful, resentful reactions that deny the achievement of the other person. This is the reality in the outer world of which everyone is a part.

An esoteric group is brought together as a result of Hierarchical necessity, soul impulse, and karmic relationship. The aspirant or disciple is a person who has one foot in the outer world and one foot in the spiritual dimension. Instead of identifying with the norm in the outer world and acting in those various kinds of negative ways, they have to learn to control these purely astral reactions. This control can only come from above, the mental plane. Aspirants and disciples therefore must learn to control their sensory, emotional reactions of spite, pride, ambition, jealousy, fear and resentment from a mental level.

Through the mental body, the soul can shine its light on every situation. You can ask yourself some very simple questions: is my response truly spiritual? Does it make for the cohesion and well-being of the group? Or is it personal, spiteful and negative, full of criticism of others? Common sense and honesty will give you the answers to these questions. The mind will give you the common sense, but if there is no honesty of mind you will not see the reaction as glamour. If you do not see it as glamour, it will never go away.

I think it necessary to set up certain conventions in every group. The first should be that the expression between all members of the group should be one of goodwill. Resentments and hatreds must be put out of the window. Jealousies and longstanding resentments are very harmful for a group, but they exist in every group. Criticism, likewise, should be seen to be destructive. It harms the person who is criticized; it harms the person who does the criticism, and it harms the group as a whole.

Encounters with Masters

Most people in the groups have had an experience of Maitreya in one form or another, but only a very small number have actually written them in and had them confirmed by my Master or even remembered or recognized them for what they were. Those who have had experiences, and had them confirmed as genuine experiences from Maitreya or one of the Masters, usually react in one of two ways. Some are filled with glamour at being so 'special' as to have a contact with the World Teacher, Maitreya. If they have several such experiences, they believe they must be very special indeed. Others, approaching it differently, think: "It could not be true. I cannot believe that it would be Maitreya because I am not worthy of having such an experience."

Both of these reactions are the result of glamour. One, the glamour of self-denigration, is seeing oneself as lower than one is. Maitreya is giving experiences to the groups, so why not? The glamour of artificial humility and the glamour of the 'big head' are equal glamours. The glamour of putting yourself down is rather more acceptable than the glamour of pushing yourself up, but it is still glamour.

Many people have repeated experiences from Maitreya. If that gives them the feeling that they are somehow special, important, or advanced in some way, that is probably a real glamour. Very often when Maitreya gives an experience, He does so in order to point out some glamour in the person. It is not because they are so special but because they need repeated experiences to get the message.

There was recently the most obvious experience of glamour because of a misunderstanding of how Maitreya works in relation to the groups, what He is actually doing. The story published in *Share International* was the original, authentic experience. [See 'Letters to the Editor' in the Appendix (p. 161) to this chapter — "Lost ring"; "The lost ring found"; " Repeat performance".] A woman from one of the groups happened upon a stall where a man was selling home-made jewellery. She selected some jewellery, and he gave her a present of a ring. Later, she lost the ring and in the meantime it was confirmed that the man was Maitreya. She longed to find the man again to be able to replace it but the man and the stall were not anywhere to be found. A year later, she found the same man and was able to buy the same ring. On the same day, another member of the group also came upon the stall and received a present of a ring from the man. The event was confirmed by my Master as a contact with Maitreya. Maitreya was the man at the stall selling the jewellery.

Word got around that Maitreya had a stall where He sold pretty, handmade jewellery made of sea shells for almost nothing, a few hundred yen (a few US dollars). When they found that this man had a regular stall, they went there to buy up as much of this jewellery as they could. Since there was a sign on the stall saying "Jewellery repaired", they even brought their own old broken jewellery for the man to repair — thinking it was Maitreya, the World Teacher! One woman even requested to pick up her repaired jewellery not on the day he suggested, but on a day that was more convenient for her! Only the first experiences published in the magazine were with Maitreya. The rest was pure glamour on the part of the group.

Maitreya's many guises

Sometimes Maitreya appears in a form which is very like how He is, as He appeared in Nairobi, Kenya, for example, when He was photographed. The clothes will be different, but the face will be more or less the same.

Or He appears as someone you know, like me, for example. He appeared at my last lecture in New York. A woman there saw me arrive in the lobby of the hotel where the lecture was scheduled. I took the lift to the top floor, where the lecture was being held. A minute afterwards she saw me come down again, walk past her, go out of the building and into the street. But of course, I did not do that. I stayed in the lecture hall and gave the lecture. She said I came down again and walked out, that it was me, no doubt about it. *Except that it was Maitreya.* He often takes someone as a pattern for a 'familiar'. She said: "I got a shock. My hair stood on end. I got 'goose pimples.' When I saw you coming down again, I thought: 'What is he coming down again for?'" It was Maitreya looking like me in every respect.

He did the same thing to a Belgian couple I know. He got on a bus after them and sat opposite them. They looked in astonishment at me sitting opposite them — except that I was black! Or sometimes He is like me only much taller. That is the hint He is giving you to recognize Him.

Most often He will appear in any form — an old man, a young man, an old woman, a young woman, even a child — where it takes your intuition to recognize Him. In many of those cases, although He is very different — a man, a woman, a fairly ordinary man — He does something unusual. Coming to one of the lectures, perhaps, and making sure He is recognized by behaving strangely, as He did recently in Osaka (Japan), singing: "I am an ordinary man from the countryside. I am totally out of place in these surroundings." Or pretending to be so drunk that He can hardly stand up, and dropping all His things out of His pocket, picking them up and dropping them again. And yet getting from one place to another like lightning. These are indications that this man is not what he seems.

These seemingly real people are 'familiars', thoughtforms deliberately created by Maitreya's imagination as a man, woman, child, perhaps a strange or funny person. In a few cases, He creates the thoughtform in the exact likeness of a real person. If you saw them together, you would see that they were absolutely alike but there would be a difference in feeling. One would be special, the other would be the ordinary person. I know several cases in which this was done. The average person in a group should be able to tell the difference because although the thoughtform and the real person look alike, the difference is that the thoughtform is informed by Maitreya's consciousness and the real person is not.

This is where the group involved with the jeweller made the mistake. The first time He was seen was Maitreya's complete visualization of the man, the stall, his companion, the jewellery, and so on. Every other contact was with the jeweller himself, not Maitreya. The group glamour got involved therefore.

Maitreya has said: "Do not run after Me. Do not claim Me. Do not try to put Me in your pocket. If you do, you will lose Me." But the group forgot that, thinking: "You got that from Maitreya? I want the same. I want some too. It is from Maitreya, with all His energy on it." So they all went running to buy jewellery. The business of the jeweller prospered, and the jewellery got more and more expensive!

That is the glamour of not recognizing the difference between Maitreya and the man on whom He was basing His thoughtform. The mistake of the group is not important, but what is important is the resulting glamorous reaction from other members of the group. Personal resentments, jealousies and accusations have come about, which are without basis —

accusations against people who have nothing to do with the entire process, or were simply caught up in the general hysteria.

Why do you think Maitreya set up this stall, this illusion of the jeweller? There has to be a reason. He would know the reaction in advance. Do you think He was just playing a trick on the group, having those women buying masses of jewellery? No, it is a lesson to the groups about the reality of the consumer society. In every nation there are those who just love to buy, buy, buy. Outside Japan the Japanese people have the reputation of loving to buy, buy, buy. It is partly to do with the social structure of present-giving, so people are always buying to give presents. Over the last 20 years or so, there has been a tremendous economic expansion in Japan due to consumerism. It is part of the consumerist society in which we live, and in which many Japanese people are caught up. This is what Maitreya is pointing out.

If someone is very prejudiced against drinking, they may have an experience of Maitreya drinking beer or seeming to be very drunk. Then they find out it is Maitreya, or recognize Him. They think: "Why does He appear as a drunk or drinking? Maybe I should be a little bit more tolerant about drinking." Or they have a big prejudice against smoking and have to share a taxi with someone who is lighting one cigarette after the other. They think: "How can I sit beside someone who is smelling so much of tobacco? I hate it." Then they find that the person has no smell of tobacco even though he has smoked 10 cigarettes. Again, a hint to be more tolerant. In the case of the jewels, if you can get this pretty, home-made jewellery for a few hundred yen, you do not have to go out and buy it all up. It is a test.

The need for spiritual intuition

There is an instance of an appearance of the Master Jesus to a woman in one of the [Japanese] groups which lasted for a month. The Master Jesus introduced Himself not as the Master Jesus, but as someone else, and finally asked permission to stay in that person's flat, used for Transmission Meditation. He gave very definite enlightenment to some of the group. [See 'Letters to the Editor' in appendix to this chapter — "House guest".]

There are two important things to recognize from a glamour point of view here. Obviously you do not open your door to just anybody. You do not invite anybody you meet for the first time to come and live with you, share your office or whatever, without some good reason, without them having given you some impression of sincerity and value. Of course, there are confidence tricksters who are so clever, so experienced, that the most aware person in the world could still be taken in. In this particular case there must have been something about the Master Jesus which was not just ordinary. The person involved had the intuition, the insight, to recognize this. The question arises: why did the others in the group not have the insight into the true nature of this man? Were they thinking like ordinary people, thinking that people are always playing confidence tricks? In other words, going along with the outer form, the outer idea and conception of people, which nine times out of 10 might be the sensible thing to do. When it was the Master Jesus, as it turned out to be, there had to be some other quality that gave the person involved the trust to invite Him to stay. He stayed for a month and left her a letter.

This sense of spiritual intuition or insight is something which everyone has to cultivate so that you know what to trust, and what is not trustworthy. The key is the heart; you can trust the heart. Your mind will give you all sorts of ideas arising out of where you come from, how you were brought up, but the heart will always tell you what is true and what is false. The glamour, of course, of the other people in the group is very clear. They tried very hard to influence her and finally succeeded. She followed her heart, and so she did the right

146

thing. She did the wrong thing by throwing away the letter that he gave her after the others' ideas were imposed on her — but she had kept it for two years.

Glamour is, as the Master Djwhal Khul has written, a world problem — the most important and difficult problem facing humanity. It is at the basis of all our pain, suffering and misdeeds, and the sooner humanity as a whole can clear away the fogs of glamour, the sooner will it progress in its evolution. (*Share International,* January/February 2000)

Within your hands, My friends, rests the key to this Appearance.
Make known the fact of My Presence among you and speed My emergence.
Far and wide make known this Truth and gather to Me your brothers and sisters.

When you see and hear Me you will realize that you have known for long the Truths which I utter.
Within your hearts rests the Truth of God.
These simple Truths, My friends, underlie all existence.

Sharing and Justice, Brotherhood and Freedom are not new concepts.
From the dawn of time mankind has linked his aspiration to these beckoning stars.
Now, My friends, shall we anchor them in the world.

From Message No. 105 – 5 June 1980

EXPLOSION OF GLAMOUR

QUESTIONS AND ANSWERS

[Questions without publication date are from the 1999 conferences in the US and Japan and were published in Share International in January/February 2000.]

Heart Response versus Mental Response

You said that the mind always rationalizes things and the heart tells the truth, that the response from the heart is always correct and to trust your heart. How can we distinguish what is coming from the heart and what from the mind?

The mind works through the brain, and you can tell whether your response is from the heart or the brain because the brain rationalizes, whereas the heart intuits. If you want to know what your heart is saying, place your attention at the heart *at the right-hand side of the body* (not the physical heart) which is the seat of the soul in the body. If you find a response there, you will know the answer, yes or no, right or wrong.

If you are experiencing from the solar plexus, that is no more trustworthy than the brain. You can always tell the difference (once you recognize it) between the solar plexus, astral/emotional reaction, and the heart reaction. These are two distinct sensations. If it is at the solar plexus, recognize it and ignore it. If you arrive at an answer from your brain by deduction — putting on the one side this and the other side that and comparing the two — you may or may not arrive at a right answer. If you experience what is happening at the heart, that reaction you can trust. It will give you the intuition that this is right to do and that is not right to do.

149

You will always find that the heart reaction is completely impersonal, objective. It does not involve your likes and dislikes. It is altruistic, non-critical. If criticism, personality differences, likes and dislikes are involved, you know that it is not from the heart. If it is from the heart, you get an intuition of clear precision but a correct decision or realization may still be fraught with difficulties. If it is against your natural personality inclination, if it is difficult and if it is a clear-cut intention of right action, then you can trust it. If it is, for example, for the good of the world, the good of society, the good of the group, even if it is unpleasant for you as a personality, then it is likely to be coming from the heart rather than the mind.

The soul, working through the heart, is not trying to turn the personality into a masochist, but so often the intentions and impulses of the soul are at variance with the likes and dislikes of the personality. You will find the prompting of the heart is always impersonal, objective, nothing to do with your likes and dislikes.

(1) Is there a difference between 'emotion' and 'feeling'? (2) I would say that emotion is astral whereas I would see feeling as being from the heart? (May 1997)

(1) Yes. (2) I would agree — if you know how to separate the two and recognize the difference.

I understand that glamour is like a fog on the astral plane. What is the relationship between glamour and the mind? There is also talk about honesty of mind. Can you make that connection?

The problem for most people is that we have no honesty of mind. We think one thing, say something else, and do something else again. So how can you trust the mind? You can only trust the mind if there is honesty of mind. There is always honesty of heart, but the person may or may not recognize it. So people try to solve their problems from the mind. But the mind works through the brain, and the person is then confused over what they really want to do or think or believe because there is no honesty of mind. There never has been. And so there is no continuity of trust in the mind.

The mind that is honest can reflect the light of the soul. The soul uses the mental body, the mind, to show the reality which the fogs of glamour prevent us from seeing. This gradually produces a degree of mental illumination on the problems of glamour, and achieves, eventually, mental polarization. There is a shift from astral to mental polarization and, in due course, to spiritual polarization.

Are honesty of mind and awareness of the heart the same?

No. They are two different ways of approaching reality. The mind, of course, has awareness. It is through the mind that the soul can see the actions of the astral body and throw its light on the glamours of the astral plane. But if you do not have honesty of mind, you do not look at the astral events, your feelings, objectively. You look at them in a biased way, to make you feel good. That is the self-deception.

Will the awareness of the heart lead to dissipation of glamour?

Honesty of mind and the awareness of the heart will lead to the dissipation of glamour. Anything that makes you more detached, which these two functions do, dissipates glamour. Glamour and detachment are opposites.

How do you distinguish between intuition and instinctive, emotional response?

Most people approach everything in a conditioned, habitual way of thought, conditioned by their prejudices, which inhibit the function of the intuition. Intuition is a function of the soul, by which the soul-light is thrown onto the mental body, and the mental body can look at the various requirements of attention. Something comes up, the person looks at it, and they have to react in one way or another. The normal, average, way is to react in the way they did yesterday, or a year ago, the way they normally do, conditioned by their prejudices, their conceptions about the nature of life. They make a quick decision, a quick thought, and it is almost always an astral/emotional reaction, not intuition at all.

A decision has to be made, and you bring to it what you are at that point. You are always more than you know but usually most people bring their habitual thought processes to bear on any situation. These, unless the person is mentally polarized, are going to be considerably conditioned by their astral imagination, their usual astral/emotional reaction to any impression and experience. The intuition hardly has a moment in which to make its contribution to the situation.

Running after Maitreya

I should probably focus my attention more on what I can do to get the word out instead of always looking around trying to recognize an experience of Maitreya. When I am not focused on seeing Maitreya, and forget myself, I find myself doing something good for this work.

Obviously everyone connected with this work would like an experience of Maitreya. So much so that I know people who are looking for an experience all the time. Every time they pass a homeless person they think: "Maybe that is Maitreya?" They concentrate on it all the time, and, of course, mostly they do not have an experience.

On the other hand, there are those who may need an experience, who are in despair, or very sick or unhappy. Maitreya or the Master Jesus may appear to them to give them hope, lift them up, make them feel better about life. I know many people who have had experiences of this kind, even 10 or 15 years ago, before they ever heard about Maitreya. The Masters know who is going to get involved in this work long before they actually get involved. The people suddenly remember the experience years later when, as we say, 'the penny drops'. They suddenly become aware of a person or experience which was unlike anything they had known before — very often at periods of stress, difficulty, deep depression and sadness.

I quite agree that it is better just to get on with the work, and if you have an experience so much the better. But to go on longing, desiring an experience from Maitreya is a waste of your time and energy. It deflects you from the real thing, which is preparing the public to recognize Maitreya. This is another way of 'running after Him.'

I know a man who lived in London, who had the most extraordinary contacts and experiences from Maitreya. (I know people who would give an arm to have just one of his experiences.) Yet despite that, and the closest contact with Maitreya, almost daily, and with the swamis with whom Maitreya works, he still ran after Maitreya. He tried to photograph Him, bribed people looking after the temples to tell him when Maitreya would be there, and would get his friends to come and photograph Him. He did not need to do this; he was seeing Maitreya all the time, but he was trying to help his friends. He never got a photograph; the camera always jammed. I warned him: "If you chase Him like this, you will get further and further away from Him." That is exactly what happened.

The more you chase Him the further He will be from you. You have to be detached even about Maitreya. Even if I know where He is I never go near the place. If I know He is going to be at a meeting, I would never go to that meeting. He is either real for you in the heart or He is not. If He is in your heart, you do not need to see Him or shake His hand.

Rays and Glamours

To recognize our glamours objectively, don't we need to know our ray structure and how the glamours are expressed?

All the rays have their particular glamours. Some have more than others, and they are all equally pernicious. The rays with the most severe glamours, the biggest number, are the 6th, 2nd and 1st rays.

The major glamours of the 1st ray are a sense of superiority, wilfulness, an exaggerated sense of one's own importance, and a separativeness as a result of these glamours. The 1st-ray type is often rather arrogant. The major glamour, therefore, of that type is pride.

The 2nd-ray glamours are usually those of self-denigration, putting oneself down. Because the 2nd-ray type often finds it difficult to handle situations in the outside world, they tend to be timid in relation to others. In its extreme form, they become like carpets to be walked over. One of the glamours of the 2nd-ray type is that they can never make up their mind. They have a great deal of empathy and can see around every subject. Because of their empathy, they tend not to have a mind of their own because they can always see the other's point of view. Empathy is a wonderful thing, but if you end up having no point of view of your own, you become rather useless in a group situation because you are always changing your mind. Timidity and aloofness are typical vices of this ray.

The 6th ray is the most glamoured of all the rays. It has the characteristics of arrogance and pride of the 1st ray —

willpower, ambition, and thrust for power — and mistakes these qualities for will. It is really desire writ large. Because the desire is so strong, it is believed to be will. Every person, probably without exception, who has given me their rays to confirm, if they have a double-6 personality (6 on the main ray and 6 on the sub-ray), believe they have a 1st-ray personality. They always mistake it for a 1st because they are so aware in themselves of this desire principle — only they call it will.

The 1st-ray type acts in a powerful way without even being aware of it. They do not think in terms of power. They just do it. The will acts, and it is a completely different type of action from the desire principle of the 6th ray. Therefore, the 1st ray, except in a relatively evolved individual, can be dangerous because it can be very destructive. The 1st-ray type, even at a high level, often has pride, but also a breadth of vision and an ability to see the bigger picture which other ray types do not.

The 6th-ray type, because of their powerful energy of desire, can do almost anything if they desire it enough. They could find their way from New York to San Francisco over the Rocky Mountains when there were no tracks, with fierce warriors with bows and arrows firing at them all the time. They are great zealots.

The 1st ray has no fear. The 1st-ray type acts without fear because they do not even think about fear. The 6th ray has powerful, energetic action without fear because their desire is so strong they overcome the fear. Most of the people in the Reappearance groups around the world have a lot of 6th ray; otherwise they would not be in the groups. They have a marked idealism, and they respond to the idea of a cause, and become devoted to that cause. That idealism is necessary in preparing the way for Maitreya. You have to respond to the idea before you can be fired up enough to do anything about it.

Although very energetic and idealistic, very ready to act bravely, the 6th-ray type often cannot work with a group. They are an extremely separative type. This causes most of the problems in the groups. They can do all sorts of work *for* the group, but they find it difficult to work *with* the group as an ordinary member at the same level as everyone else. They are highly individualistic but find it hard to put their individuality at the service of the group.

This type thinks everyone in the group is wrong except them, that they know better than every one else. There is often a constant fight between people of that type and the group as a whole. This is found all over the world. Such individuals should not be given positions of power in a group because they often misuse it. They seldom understand group need, group good, and the work for that, except on their own terms. Self-deception is a major vice of this type.

The 3rd-ray type has many glamours, the chief of which is an over-capacity for rationalization. The 3rd ray, especially when it is on the mental plane, rationalizes everything. Every action, every reaction, is rationalized until the person feels comfortable, so there is a marked dishonesty in the 3rd-ray type. The 3rd ray type tends to be the 'spider at the centre of the web'. Such a person likes to have a finger in every pie. They manipulate and create little cliques of their friends whom they can influence. They have no real sense of group awareness or consciousness. They are good at making money and can manipulate the outer physical world rather well, but in terms of spiritual consciousness they are limited. They tend to be active for action's sake — they cannot sit still.

The 2nd ray is the opposite. The 2nd-ray type has very quick, easy contact with the soul without any effort, and so they become rather introverted. This means that on the outer physical plane they may be handicapped. They do not find that easy. The

3rd-ray types find the outer physical plane very easy to control but find soul-contact difficult indeed.

The 5th-ray type, especially those with the 5th ray on the mind and the physical-brain level, are so withdrawn into the mental plane that they are very critical of those who do not see what they see. They see clearly, but in a very limited way, on a very narrow range. They are rather arrogant about their ability to see clearly, forgetting about the world of which they see nothing at all which exists outside their limited viewpoint. Many scientists are very influenced by the 5th ray. Modern technology is a 5th-ray phenomenon. There is a very sharp, clear insight into a small area and a complete lack of awareness of the bigger world, the world of different levels of consciousness. Most scientists are against any esoteric viewpoint at all. It never occurs to them that there is more to the world than they can see in the microscope and measure.

The glamours or vices of the 4th-ray are many. They are summarized by the Master Djwhal Khul (through Alice Bailey) as Self-centredness (to which I would add exhibitionism — communication 'gone over-the-top'. Many well known entertainers and pop artists have double 4th ray — major and sub-ray — on the personality); worrying, inaccuracy, lack of moral courage, strong passions, indolence, extravagance. I would add procrastination and self-dramatizing.

Seventh-ray glamours are given by the Master Djwhal Khul as formalism, bigotry, pride, narrowness, superficial judgements, self-opinion over-indulged. I would add a marked inflexibility and remoteness.

All these ray-types have virtues; I am talking only about the glamours. We do not need to talk about the virtues because they will always be positive. The glamours, the vices, are the destructive tendencies.

With the Master Djwhal Khul's comment in mind about the 6th-ray type taking the place of power and authority, I have consciously made myself always co-operate from behind the group, and be impersonal instead of taking the lead, due to my ray structure. I assume this is because it is powerfully 6th ray in its make-up.

One of the major glamours of the 6th-ray type is self-deception. The 6th-ray type is very idealistic indeed. But they mistake the ideal for the performance. I do not believe it if a 6th-ray type says: "I know my possible faults. I know I will want to dominate and control the group, so I will stand behind and not push myself forward. I will work from behind the scenes and not be very forthcoming." I do not know the person involved so I cannot tell you whether I am right or wrong. That is the intention, I am sure, but I would bet my bottom dollar that it is not the fact. It is the self-deception of the 6th ray.

Let us take an objective example outside the group or personalities. Take the United States of America — 2nd-ray soul, 6th-ray personality. The ideal of the USA is that it sees the brotherhood of man. It sees itself as the upholder of peace, justice and freedom everywhere in the world. It really has that ideal. Everyone 'knows' that an American is 'free' and 'liberated' better than anyone else. Ask any American, and you will get that response. "Yes, we believe in justice. We believe in freedom for everybody." Black and white? "Yes, black and white." Ask a black American, especially in the South, if he feels free. Does he feel he has justice? You will get a very different answer. There are Americans, and there are other Americans.

Since World War II, America has invaded more countries than any other nation — from South Korea and Vietnam onwards. If they have not actually invaded a country, they have subverted it by aiding rebels within it — working through groups, giving them arms and money. That is what the CIA is for, to subvert other nations.

That is the reality, but the *ideal* is justice and freedom for everyone, US-style. There are around 265 million people in the United States, and, officially, 33 million people live below the poverty line. That is the most blatant self-deception, and is the result of this 6th-ray tendency.

Likewise, the person who wrote this question, I believe, feels: "I have a lot of 6th ray. I know the Master Djwhal Khul says that they should not be given power and authority because they always misuse it, so I will stay behind the scenes. That would be the best and honest thing for me to do." Because they have the idea, they think that is what they are actually doing. They seldom carry out the ideal. You have to be a very advanced type actually to carry on the ideal.

Why would a 6th-ray soul give its vehicle a 6th-ray personality, 6th-ray astral body, and maybe a 6th-ray mind as well?

It very often happens — sometimes double 6, double 6, double 6. I know people with that ray structure. It is done to bring the whole matter to a head so that in a particular incarnation when the person has reached some degree of evolution, maybe somewhere between 1 and 1.5, they are able to recognize glamour when they see it written in big letters. The soul gives those ray structures with such an emphasis to make the glamours so obvious that even that type can recognize it at last, after all those incarnations in which they were in a fog. They can begin to see because their glamours are so strong, so clear cut.

Why does the soul place its focus on the 6th-ray personality when the 6th ray has such glamour?

My experience is that most often the soul focus is on the mental body in order that the person, in that life or the next, may achieve mental polarization. If the soul-focus is on the personality 6th ray, it may be, as I said before, to make the glamours so obvious that the person sees them. And, hopefully, to allow the perfection of the soul to reflect itself through the 6th-ray personality. The outstanding virtue of the 6th ray, which, of course, the soul has, is self-sacrifice. That does not mean that the 6th-ray personality has, necessarily, a strong capacity for self-sacrifice. If they are advanced they would, but that is not always the case. If you take the higher qualities, the virtues of the 6th ray — self-sacrifice, vision, the ability to envision the ideal, idealism, devotion, one-pointedness, loyalty — and turn them into their opposites, you have the vices of the 6th ray. Instead of loyalty you get the Judas, disloyalty. Instead of vision you get self-deception. Instead of devotion you get blind devotion for a certain time and then at times the extreme opposite. Separatism is the big vice of the 6th ray.

Everyone knows the type. Every group has it: a person who is full of ideals for, and about, the group, but cannot work with, only for, the group. They cannot work with other people, cannot see themselves at the level of other people and work with them. They always know better, so they cannot work with anyone. I exaggerate, of course, but that is the tendency.

Until you see glamour as unreal, you cannot do anything about it. You are in it and that is all you can do. So the soul will emphasize the possibility of glamours in the personality or astral body, sometimes the mental body, in order to bring the glamours forward, make them so big and obvious that the person will at last see them for what they are.

What is the role of the 1st ray within co-operative relationships, especially regarding leadership? (May 1998)

That question, to my mind, is a demonstration of a wrong idea most 2nd- or 6th-ray people have about what the 1st ray is like. The 1st-ray person is always thought to be a leader, and certainly very many 1st-ray people have leadership qualities. This quality, however, is not exclusive to the 1st ray. If that were the case, there would be relatively very few leaders in the world, because there are relatively very few 1st-ray souls in the world. And since we are in a 2nd-ray solar system, that 1st ray is always the first sub-ray of the 2nd ray. There is no pure 1st ray in this solar system.

The 1st ray is always taken to be the one who drives forward with total fearlessness, makes a great leader, inspires others. That can be, and often is, the case. Hitler was such a person, but did it do any good for the world? It did not do any good for the people of Germany, and did great harm to many millions of people. Twenty-five million people died in Russia alone fighting Hitler's armies. Six million Jews and perhaps a million Hungarians, Gypsies, Poles and other ethnic groups died in the murder camps under Hitler.

Like every other ray, the 1st ray can be destructive or constructive, but it is not the only ray for leadership. It is relatively rare in the groups that I personally know and I know the ray structure of many hundreds of people in the groups all over the world. The 1st ray is so rare that you would find very few people in those groups with a 1st-ray soul. Occasionally, you would find a 1st-ray mind. The 1st-ray personality is, luckily, relatively rare, because it is difficult to handle. A few have a 1st-ray astral. The only astral ray which I have never yet seen is a 5th ray. I have met one very, very rare 7th-ray astral. The 3rd-ray astral is, of course, also relatively rare.

The 1st-ray is a particular type of mind, a power mind, which has a broad view of things, and which can focus ideas with power and is therefore very influential. If you look at the list of initiates and their ray structures in the back of *Maitreya's Mission, Volume Three* (or the earlier volumes) you will find that an enormous number of those initiates had a 1st-ray mind. If they are great army generals or kings, you might find 1st-ray personalities as well, and very often 1st-ray physicals. A 1st-ray mind you will find in people who became very influential in their lives in whatever work they were engaged in. It does not mean to say they were leaders but they were leaders of thought. They were not necessarily political leaders, although many were — like Hitler, Tito, Mao Zedong and Winston Churchill. They all demonstrate that quality of mind.

Soul Rays

Will the ray of the soul manifest as glamour?

No, never. The soul has no glamour. Glamour results from the quality of the soul not being able to manifest purely through the personality or the vehicles.

The soul does not have glamour, but why is it that a person who does not have the soul ray in any personality rays would express the glamour of the soul ray? (JC May 2000)

The personality expresses the glamours. Although the soul does not have glamours, being perfect, the problem is that on the personality level, the glamours, which are the opposite aspects of the perfect soul quality, express themselves. That is one reason.

Another reason is that the soul ray, whatever it is, is not the source of all aspects. It shares these aspects with other rays. If you have a certain glamour, which you recognize on the personality or mental level, it may well be the opposite of the virtue of several rays, because these qualities, to quite a degree, are shared. Some 2nd-ray qualities, for example, are shared by the 4th and 6th rays. Some 1st-ray qualities are shared by the 3rd. The 3rd-ray qualities, to some extent, are shared by the 5th and the 7th rays. It is not so cut and dried as you might imagine. If you look at the list of glamours, or the virtues and vices of the different rays, you will see that certain of them have two, three or four of the same vices.

Another reason is that no one is in their first incarnation. Everyone has had all the rays over and over again as part of their equipment in different lives. These qualities are already built into the 'system'.

Which bodies — astral, mental, soul, etc — are more responsible for glamour?

You have to rule out the soul. The soul is not responsible for glamour, but the personality, astral body and mental body are all responsible for glamour. The lack of detachment of the personality is the real cause of glamour.

[For more information on the Seven Rays, see Benjamin Creme, *Maitreya's Mission, Volumes One* and *Two*.]

How the Masters Teach

Will the Masters teach us directly when They emerge? Otherwise the whole world cannot change.

The Masters are not going to run your life for you. They are not going to say: "You should be doing more of this and this and that." My Master does not do that with me. If I want to know anything, I have to ask Him. Otherwise He never says a word. And I have to ask in the right way, otherwise I may get an answer and mistake its meaning.

For instance, in the early days, if I were reading a book, and I would come on something and think I had intuitively come to the meaning, I would say: "Is that it?" And the Master would say: "Exactly, exactly." He did this for many months. I thought, I am pretty good, I understand all of this. I thought my intuition was really working. It was a long time before I realized "exactly" did not mean I was exactly right. It meant: "Exactly. That is what you are saying." Masters are very precise. He would not say: "No, no. That is wrong." That would have set me on a different tack. That would be something it was not His right to tell me. It would be an infringement of my right to teach myself. You should be teaching yourself, not asking or expecting a Master to teach you.

Will you give us some examples of how you became free of your own glamours?

I was taken in hand by my Master, and the deglamourization and disillusioning process was so intense it is very difficult for me to give you an idea. It was like going through a profound, continuous, 20-hours-a-day psychoanalysis. Not going once or twice a week to the analyst and talking for an hour in a nice cosy way, but continuously, as if He were sitting on your shoulder, going through the most painful, disillusioning deglamourization. Nonstop, minute after minute, day after day, with this voice going on in your head. Occasionally He would apologize for having to do this. You cannot get away from a Master's voice. He can make His voice louder than any thought that you can set up. He can imitate any noise in your head. He can imitate other people's voices, and it might be a few minutes before I would realize it was not that person but the Master. They can do any magical thing. I cannot begin to tell you. I would hear somebody's voice. I would know that person, and then I would have to decide whether it was true or false. I got crafty. I would say no, you missed out that time. No way would I take that for being so and so. The voice would be the same but there was something missing.

It is like showing you your every weakness in the first place, taking your weakest points and then hammering at them over and over again, until you think: "Phew, I can leave that one alone, just forget about it," after being through the mill for maybe several days all on the one thing. It was so hard, and so many years ago, I can barely remember. I know the feeling, and I know some of the things, but I cannot really give you precise instances except to say that He would take what I would see today as weakness, which at the time I might or might not have seen; but whether I saw it or not I sure got rid of it. He hammered away until I saw it from every point of view; points of view I could see, but also points of view I never even thought of, until that weakness would be clear as a bell, I could walk all around it. That way I could give it up. That could be an illusion or glamour, sometimes one and sometimes the other.

There comes a point when glamour can be conquered, but the problem changes into illusion. When it is mental, it is illusion. In practice it works out as the same.

In normal life we experience reactions that if we are aware enough we catch as a glamour at the time, but we might have to wait months before a circumstance appears where the reaction comes back to us. It seems that your Master created these circumstances and concentrated a whole lifetime of experience?

That is probably a good insight into the situation. It is as if the whole thing is telescoped, so in weeks or months one goes through the equivalent of years of the most painful and intense type of psychoanalysis. It is not psychoanalysis in the usual sense but I cannot think of another word for it. It is psychic presentation. He would just, as it were, quietly, bring up a word or idea. "Let us look at this." And then He would have me relate it to myself. So I was doing all the analysis, all the approach-work to it. He was not saying do this or that, or you are a naughty boy or a good boy. Nothing like that at all. It is presenting you to you. "Does that feel right to you? Are you happy with this? Because you have shown Me this is what you are, this is what you are like." It is like a mirror. He is showing you, and keeping on showing you, until you say: "We dealt with that yesterday." He would say: "Well, perhaps we did and perhaps we did not. Let us look at it again." "Oh, no!" Really painful. And He would apologize.

The Masters are so considerate and polite. I will say: "What's this ray structure? What's that ray structure?" I am so impolite. And He will say: "Would Creme be so kind as to ...," and I would have to remember. "Would the Master be so kind as to ...," instead of: "What's that? What's this? How many? What's the percentage?" The difference between me and the politeness of a Master is total, absolute. People ask me questions all the time, and I get into the habit of just turning to Him quickly for the answer. Even if I am alone I do it. That is shameful, terrible.

But the Master in this case apologizes. He says: "Master apologizes for putting you through this, but it is necessary, painful but necessary." It is a terrible process!

It has, however, given me the detachment necessary to do my job: to speak to any audience, large or small, about these very controversial matters, to a very sceptical world, on stage or television or radio; to be openly overshadowed by the Christ, the Lord Maitreya, and say not a word to the audience for up to an hour — and hold their rapt attention.

APPENDIX — Letters

Editor's note: Over a number of years, some of the Masters, in particular Maitreya, the Master Jesus and the Master in Tokyo, have attended Benjamin Creme's lectures and meditations; They also appear in various guises to large numbers of people, especially those involved in the work for the Reappearance. The recipients of these experiences send letters to the editor of *Share International* and if authentic — an experience from a Master — this is confirmed by Benjamin Creme's Master and published. Those that are not authentic, ie 'ordinary', remain unpublished. The spirit and morale of the groups involved in the work for the Reappearance have thus been immensely strengthened.

These experiences are given to inspire, to guide or teach, often to heal and uplift. After the experience the people, often depressed and unhappy, feel immeasurably relieved and joyful. In many appearances, and this has happened for probably hundreds of years, the Masters act as saving 'angels' — for example in accidents, during wartime, earthquakes and so on. Very often, too, They draw attention to, or comment on, in an amusing way, some fixed intolerance (for example against smoking or drinking) held by the individual involved.

They use a 'familiar', a thoughtform, who seems totally real, and through whom the Master's thoughts can be expressed. These familiars take very many forms: They can appear as a man, a woman, a child, at will. Sometimes They use the 'blueprint' of a real person, appearing in an almost identical guise to that individual. The following letters illustrate this procedure, especially in the story of the Japanese jewelry maker.

Lost ring

Dear Editor,

On my way to Transmission Meditation in April 1998, I was walking along a street near Asagaya Station in Tokyo and I noticed a street vendor selling jewelry. He was selling pendants made from seashells for 300 yen ($3) per piece. A woman was talking with him while selecting. Because they were priced so cheaply I was compelled to stop by the stall. I selected several and placed them in front of the man.

He discontinued the conversation with the woman and looked up and gazed at me. He picked out one of the pendants I selected and said: "This is an expensive one. It costs 1,800 yen ($18), but I will charge you 1,200 yen because you did not know."

Then he picked up a ring and said: "I will give this to you. Give me your hand." When I gave him my left hand, he said: "This is an expensive one. It is for your pinky (little) finger." He put it on my finger. To my surprise, it was a perfect fit, although I have quite small fingers. It was very cute and I felt happy. As I was leaving, he said: "Come again."

I have walked that street every week, but I had never seen him before and I have not seen his stall since. I remember hearing the woman who was talking to him, say: "I often buy these from you." I thought it was strange.

I kept the ring on my finger all the time even when I washed my hands, because I was afraid I might lose it. One day, for some reason, I had been concerned about the ring all day. I went to Transmission Meditation that day, and I knew I still had the ring when the Meditation was over. But on my way home, I noticed the ring was gone. I had never taken it off my finger. It was as if it just disappeared.

When the man gazed at me, his eyes reminded me of the eyes of the woman on a bicycle I saw a year ago who turned out to be Maitreya. Was this man Maitreya? If so, why did my ring disappear? Who was the woman who was talking to him?

T.K., Tokyo, Japan.

(Benjamin Creme's Master confirms that the man was Maitreya. The ring did not disappear: the writer dropped it. The 'woman' was the Master Jesus.)

The lost ring found

Dear Editor

A year ago in April 1998, I met Maitreya in the guise of a street vendor who gave me a ring and I lost it. I was quite saddened by that and deeply ashamed of my carelessness. However, I still have a pendant and a brooch I bought from him and I always wear them as talismans.

I have a chronic sense of despair in my personal life, but I also know that I could only live in the way that my soul dictates to me no matter how painful or difficult my life becomes. I have always kept Maitreya in my mind and pray to Him to give me courage.

On Friday 16 April 1999, around 5.30pm, I was again on my way to Transmission Meditation. I remembered that I met Maitreya in this area about this time last year. To my surprise, I saw the same vendor there. Instead of pendants and brooches on the stall, only the rings were displayed prominently and the price tag said 300 yen. Since I had always been thinking about my lost ring, I went straight to the ring box and began to look. There were so many rings and I couldn't figure out which one was the one I had lost. When I picked up a ring, the man said: "It has cubic zircon inlaid." And I remembered that indeed my lost ring had three small zircons inlaid in a straight line. The man said: "It is made for a pinky finger." And I remembered that it was indeed for my pinky finger. I put it on my finger and it fitted perfectly. It was exactly the ring I lost last year. The man said, smilingly, as if he knew my mind: "Now, is that OK?" I nodded deeply and purchased the ring. At that time, I was so thrilled to have the lost ring back that I did not care if the man was Maitreya or not. I was so happy that I had completely forgotten about my daughter's request to get one for her if I ever met Him again. When I looked at his eyes, he gazed at me for a moment.

They were the same grey colour as the eyes of the vendor last year.

As I stood up to leave, I noticed an old lady standing beside him. She was not there when I first saw him. Was this man Maitreya? Who was the old lady? If He was Maitreya, He has given me the sign twice. Who could hope for better encouragement than this? I have renewed my determination to have real courage and to live with faith. I will do the best I can and leave the rest in the hand of God.

T.K., Tokyo, Japan.

(Benjamin Creme's Master confirms that the man was Maitreya. The 'old lady' was the Master Jesus.)

Repeat performance

Dear Editor,

On 16 April 1999, a little past 5.15pm, near the doorway of the night-deposit of Tokyo Mitsubishi bank in Asagaya, I saw a street vendor selling jewellery. The man was wearing a Taylor collar jacket and a dark brown hat. After I finished my shopping at the nearby supermarket, I went back, and there were two other customers. I picked up a ring from a case marked 300 yen ($3), but it was so small that I was surprised and returned it to the case. (At that time, I didn't realize that it was for a pinky finger.) Then I looked at pendants. I found one with a design I liked, but I wished it were a brooch. I held it and asked the man: "This is a pendant, isn't it?" The vendor then showed me a brooch, saying: "I have this." It was exactly the same design as the pendant. "This is made of seashell front and back," he said. It had very beautiful lustre with fine lines all over.

I picked up one of the brooches shaped like a bird and asked: "Isn't this a bird?" He answered: "It's a bird, indeed. You will not find anything like this around here." I asked: "Did you make it yourself?" "I made all these myself. That's why I can sell them so cheaply." Then he showed a pair of earrings to another customer, saying: "I made this only last night." They were so beautiful that I could not help commenting on them to the woman: "They look very good on you." The woman turned to me and smiled. I was surprised at her beauty.

Then I suddenly noticed the old woman with a knitted hat sitting beside the man. I wondered when she came and asked the man: "Is she your wife?" He replied: "We have been together for 60 years now." I began to calculate in my mind and thought to myself: "That means they must be over 80 years old. Well, the man looks much younger and very energetic, but the woman does look her age." The woman was just smiling without a word and looked very serene. The man had tanned skin with lots of blemishes that looked rather artificial. He had glasses on, and his eyes were large and powerful and penetrating.

Finally I decided to buy two brooches, one at 300 yen and the other at 900 yen. When I gave him 1,200 yen, he said: "1,000 yen will do." Then he looked at me and said: "Give me your hand." I put out my right hand. He told me to give him my pinky finger, and to my surprise, he put the ring on my finger. It was a ring with three small cubic zircons inset in a row. He said: "I will give this to you." At that moment I realized I was having the same experience as my co-worker, Mrs K. The man said: "Come again." I replied: "Yes, I will."

Will you please tell me if this man was Maitreya, and who were the old woman and the outstandingly beautiful female customer?

H.N., Tokyo, Japan.

(Benjamin Creme's Master confirms that the man was Maitreya. The 'old woman' was the Master Jesus. The 'beautiful woman customer' was the Master in Tokyo.)

House guest

Dear Editor,

In the beginning of August 1995, a man came to the Kyobashi Transmission Meditation room in Osaka, Japan. He was slim and 178 cm (5ft.10ins) tall. He had wide shoulders, and short, black wavy hair. His eyes were piercing. He looked like an ordinary white-collar worker.

He had phoned me at home in advance and said: "My name is Mori. You are worrying about something now, aren't you? I can tell from the tone of your voice." And he had suggested meeting me to talk, so we arranged to meet at the Transmission room. As soon as he saw me, he told me he was glad that I looked just like the boyish woman he had imagined. While we were talking, he mentioned that he would like to experience the meditation. Then he asked if he could stay in that room for a while because he wanted to write an article. I was surprised by this request. But he did point out my problems and was kind enough to listen to me and advise me, and he did not seem to be a bad person. So I obtained the approval of the owner of the building as well as the members of the Transmission group and arranged to have him stay there for a while. (It was simply an office room with a few chairs and cushions.)

He told me about himself: that he had a home in Shizuoka city and his son and daughter were living abroad; his wife was an artist-type and pursuing various hobbies including playing the *koto* instrument, living an elegant life. He had a happy family life, but on a stormy morning he decided to leave home and roam around the world. He was successful in everything he laid hands on and established good relationships with the local people wherever he went. In one place, he made a success of baking bread, but he gave that up to someone else and went on roaming. He even gave me his business card which said he was a director of a major kimono company, and said that he had a large bank account.

I gradually began to enjoy taking care of him and looked forward to going to him every morning, bringing him breakfast. Then, he would read me the part of the manuscript he had written the day before. It had become our routine. However, when I talked about him to members of the Transmission group I was advised to be careful, that he could be a swindler, and he could be using me; that I was too kind and too trusting, etc. I told him what the group members said because I wanted to see his reaction. His expression seemed to change momentarily but we went back to our usual conversation. I left the room after about an hour.

One Saturday morning, after a Transmission, he told the group members that he would show us the experience of the Self. He made a tube with his hands and placed them in front of his eyes and said that the one who is looking is the Self and the one being seen on the other side of the tube is you. The people had been so expectant that they were very disappointed by his explanation and seemed to be convinced that he really was a fake. He also said that there was a certain colour that would best suit each person, and that white would suit me best and that I should wear more white clothes. Someone was advised to wear light purple.

One day, he said that our activities have to be made known more widely and that he was intending to complete his manuscript and publish it in a book. He had a friend who was an editor, etc. He also said he intended to go to Tokyo to meet Mrs T.I., a co-worker of Share Japan, and also to London to meet Benjamin Creme.

One month later, he suddenly left, leaving behind a letter for me. The content of the letter was to do with Jesus's three temptations in the wilderness. There was no more communication from him after that, and I did not hear about Mrs T.I. meeting him, nor about the publication of his book. So I thought perhaps he really was a swindler and threw away his letter which I had been keeping for about two years like a talisman for my spiritual support.

I have mostly forgotten the content of the letter but it included the following:

The first temptation:

Devil: If you are the Son of God, command these stones to become loaves of bread.

Jesus: Man shall not live by bread alone.

The second temptation:

If you are the Son of God, throw yourself down from here and your God will save you before you strike your foot against a stone.

Jesus: Man shall not test his Lord.

The third temptation:

Devil: I will give you all the kingdoms of the world and the glory of them, if you worship me.

Jesus: You shall worship the Lord your God and Him only shall you serve.

At the end of the letter, it said: "Thank you very much. I shall not forget you. I look forward to seeing you again in future. With love."

They were written on two pages of a 400-word manuscript with a strong, quite characteristic handwriting.

When I think about him now, I sometimes wonder if he could have been a Master. Although I was 99.9 per cent doubtful some part of me has kept nagging at me about him and I finally decided to inquire. Although everyone thought he was a fake, I could not doubt the fact that he did help me divert my attention from the personal problem I was facing at the time and gave me very important spiritual support. I suppose I threw away the letter when I became strong enough not to need the psychological crutch any longer.

If he was a Master, I believe He did keep his promise. He came back (in a different guise) to visit the Kyobashi Transmission room two years later, in April 1997, one week before Easter, and talked with me for about 30 minutes and meditated with the group for three hours. [Ref: the letter entitled "A promise is a promise", *Share International*, September 1998. See below.]

PS: By the way, we used to have two chairs in the Meditation room, but at some point in time those chairs disappeared from the room and nobody knows what happened to them. Is there any significance to the disappearance of the chairs?

N.M. Osaka, Japan.

(Benjamin Creme's Master confirms that the man was the Master Jesus. He made the chairs disappear because He had sat on them a lot, and they were over-charged for ordinary members of the group.)

A Promise is a Promise

Dear Editors,

On a Saturday morning in April 1997, one week before Easter, I went to the Kyobashi (Osaka, Japan) Transmission Meditation room about 30 minutes earlier than everyone else. A man came into the room and asked to take part in the Transmission. I asked him if he had done Transmission Meditation before and he said: "Yes, at an apartment at Temmabashi." Remembering that there used to be a Transmission group there, I said to him that he must already know how to do Transmission. He then walked over to the tetrahedron and asked: "What kind of instrument is this?"

Rather than taking the chance of giving him an inaccurate explanation, I opened the book on Transmission Meditation, to the page where the tetrahedron is explained, and asked him to read it.

Then he sat down in front of the potted plants in the room and began to talk to me. He had a hairstyle that reminded me of an artist, and I thought to myself that he had the air of a single man. He said: "I am single." I thought to myself he must be in his late 30s. Then he said: "I am 40 years old." I asked him where he lived. He said: "Tezukayama." I chuckled unwittingly, and playfully slapped his shoulder, saying: "That's why you are still single at the age of 40!" (Tezukayama is a part of Osaka where rich people live and I thought he must be a son of a wealthy family.) He just smiled.

Soon other members arrived and we began the meditation at 10am and finished at 12 noon. He meditated with us for two hours. Afterwards he said he was planning to go to the Prema (the other Transmission Meditation centre in Osaka). So I asked him to relay a message that there would be a 24-hour Easter Transmission Meditation at the Kyobashi room a week later. We all went outside and discussed where to place posters of Benjamin Creme's up-coming lecture. The man was still with us, listening to our conversation with a smile on his face. I told him: "You don't need to stay any more. You may go home."

Later, I asked the Prema people if they received the message. I was told that the message was written on the blackboard but they did not see the man. He kept this promise but he was never seen again at any Transmission groups after that. Who was the man?

N.M., Osaka, Japan.

(Benjamin Creme's Master confirms that the man was the Master Jesus.)

My dear friends, I am happy to be with you once more.

My Plan is that My Teaching should precede My Presence and prepare My way. My people will release it through their groups and group endeavour. When mankind is somewhat prepared My voice shall be heard.

Meanwhile, My efforts are bearing fruit, producing change, drawing together men and nations, and bringing new hope to the world. I am emerging soon, but first I would point the way into the new direction which Man, if he would survive, must take.

Firstly, men must see themselves as brothers, sons of the One Father. This is essential if they would progress one step nearer The Godhead.

Throughout the world there are men, women and little children who have not even the essentials to stay alive; they crowd the cities of many of the poorest countries in the world. This crime fills Me with shame.

My brothers, how can you watch these people die before your eyes and call yourselves men?

My Plan is to save these, My little ones, from certain starvation and needless death.

My Plan is to show you that the way out of your problems is to listen again to the true voice of God within your hearts, to share the produce of this most bountiful of worlds among your brothers and sisters everywhere.

I need your help, I call on you to aid Me in My task.

How can I stand aside and watch this slaughter, watch My little ones die? No, My friends, this cannot be.

Therefore I am come quickly among you once more to show you the way, point the path.

But the success of My Mission depends on you: you must make the choice — whether you share and learn to live peacefully as true men, or perish utterly.

My heart tells Me your answer, your choice, and is glad.

Message No. 11 – 5 January 1978

PART THREE

UNITY

THE NEED FOR UNITY

by the Master —, through Benjamin Creme

Unity must be sought for with all diligence. In unity there is not only strength but beauty. Cultivate unity as a wise gardener cultivates his garden, tending carefully each new bud and shoot. Unity follows every true manifestation of love and graces each achievement of the spirit.

Take unity as your banner and walk the way of power. Unity makes all things possible. Without unity nothing is certain; the finest possibilities come to dust. Achievement lies in the right use of the given capacities; lacking unity, the highest potential may be wasted.

Invincible

Unity is a manifestation of spirit, for the true nature of humanity is One. All that leads to unity benefits the race and lends wings to the journey. Unity is invincible; the dark ones beat on the shield of unity in vain. The time is coming when unity will be achieved but the first steps in that direction must be taken now. Useless it is to wait for others to start; the move towards unity must be made by each one. Nothing so pierces the web of unity as criticism.

A thousand possibilities are lost in this way. Keep silent the tongue of criticism and protect the precious fabric so carefully spun.

Each in his own way knows the power of unity; each seeks from his neighbour approval and consent, but mechanical conformity of thought here has no place. Each move in the direction of unity adds power to the whole and lightens the task of the Toilers behind the scenes. Create unity and know the true nature of man. Preserve unity and allow the spirit of man to flourish. Teach unity and unleash the love in your brother's heart.

Peace

If humanity would know peace it must see itself as One. Nothing less will take it to that blessed state. Peace will be established when justice rules and the poor no longer beg for mercy. Without justice, unity is unthinkable and would for ever evade man's grasp. Establish, then, the rule of justice and bring unity and peace to this anguished world.

Through sharing alone will justice be confirmed. Sharing alone will bring the peace desired by all the nations. When men share and destroy the walls of separation they will know at last the truth of their existence and flood the world with brotherhood and love.

Take sharing as your guide into the future. Release your brothers from the grip of poverty and pain. Open yourselves to the impulses of the soul and establish in your midst the Will of God.

Sacrifice

God's Will, We affirm, will be established. Through unity and love men will come to share. Through sacrifice and reason men will find the way to justice and peace. Freedom and brotherhood await man's action. All can be achieved.

Together, men can perform all manner of mighty deeds. Limitless are the possibilities of change, but men must act together to create the new world. Through unity alone will men conquer. The strength of unity will open all gates. Hold fast to the ideal of brotherhood and cease to mock your brother's efforts. Know that he, too, faces the storm and struggles in the dark.

A new Light

Since man was, man has fought. Always have the cleavages been known. Today there enters a new Light into the lives of men to cleanse the world of bigotry and war. Help to spread the Light of sanity and peace. Help to create the ways of justice and freedom. Work to build the unity which will see men through and gather them together under the banner of the Christ.

The future must be won. All hands are needed for the work. Let the inner union manifest and join hands together for the task. (*Share International*, September 1984)

UNITY

by the Master —, through Benjamin Creme

Whenever men meet together in large groups they adopt a different view of themselves and look at each other in a new way. They are emboldened, strengthened in their desire and gravitate to those who support their viewpoint. This may seem natural but why should it be so?

Essentially, all men inwardly seek unity and find its reflection in conformity of thought and ideas. This instinct is behind the formation of political parties and other groups. The ideological consensus acts as a magnet and strengthens the potency of the whole.

Groups and parties founder when the inner unity is disturbed. Unity is a soul quality and essential for the cohesion of the group. Too great an emphasis on individuals and personality differences thus tends to weaken the unifying ties which hold the group together.

This principle can be seen at work in every branch of human activity. The rise and fall of parties, groups and even of nations are conditioned by this law. Unity is strength, say men, and thus it is, for it is man's essential nature.

Unity is not too difficult to attain in the earlier stages of formation of a group; if the purpose of its inception is magnetic enough, that alone can hold the group together. However, time brings differences and discontent. Strong and varied voices arise and seek to impose their will. If the *desire* for unity is lost the group, at once, is threatened.

Interconnectedness

The underlying purpose of all life is the creation of unity, thus expressing the interconnectedness of all atoms. For most men, cosmos is a collection of separate material bodies, infinitely large and distant, inertly obeying mechanical laws of matter. In reality, Cosmos, Space Itself, is a living entity, the Source of our Being, our Mother and Father. As souls, we know this to be so, and seek to give expression to the fundamental unity of our nature.

A group, therefore, loses this unity at its peril. Without such unity it functions not as a group but blindly, without purpose and cohesion, a disparate collection of attitudes and conditioning.

Aquarius

We are entering the Age of the Group; Aquarius, and its energies, can be lived and experienced only in group formation. The major quality of Aquarius, too, is Synthesis. Its fusing and blending rays will impose themselves on the lives of all until, gradually, the higher alchemy achieves its beneficent purpose and the race of men are One. Thus will it be. Thus will men know the truth that Unity *is* strength, the essential nature of our Being, the purpose to which all men strive and to which all activities of men seek to give expression.

When Maitreya, Himself, emerges in the very near future, He will underline the need for unity in all our undertakings. He will show how essential it is that we find an identity of purpose, as men and as nations, in solving human problems, thus putting our potent individualities at the service of the group. (*Share International*, July/August 2001)

UNITY — THE AIM OF LIFE

[The following article is an edited version of the keynote talk given by Benjamin Creme at the Transmission Meditation Conference held near San Francisco, USA, in July 2001.]

I have decided to take one of the most important subjects for this keynote talk. Everyone attending this conference thinks about the keynote talk and makes it the subject of their focus, meditation and contemplation for the whole of the weekend. And bit-by-bit they put it into their lives throughout the rest of the year. That is the ideal. Of course, the ideal is seldom achieved but something approaching that, perhaps, will come out of our investigations.

I have chosen the subject of unity. I use in the first place the article on unity that my Master wrote for the July/August 2001 issue of *Share International,* because it is probably one of the most profound statements that could be made by anyone.

I have looked through some of the articles in *A Master Speaks* and found another article on unity — 'The Need for Unity', which my Master wrote in September 1984. It is an extraordinary article. He talks about the same subject from another point of view. The variety of approach and the richness in these two versions are quite extraordinary. I think only a Master's mind could approach a subject like that from such a full and substantial, abstract and yet practical, standpoint.

The need for unity

"Unity must be sought for with all diligence." That gives one the impression, does it not, that unity is not something which happens of its own accord, by chance. It is not automatic.

"In unity there is not only strength but beauty," something more than strength, something that is achieving that beauty which suggests that it is made in the framework of the divine idea. Beauty is an expression of a divine idea, and when our expression achieves the revelation of the idea, beauty is created. This is behind all the great art, music, poetry and literature; all the great scientific discoveries in the world; all the great intuitions, in religious terms, about the nature of the reality in which we live. All of that achieves a beauty, a divine radiation, which is only to be found when you are touching the highest, most mysterious parts of life. When you are thinking in terms of the meaning and purpose of life, beauty results.

Likewise, unity achieves beauty because it reflects a divine purpose. If it is true to say that the purpose of all life is the creation of unity, then indeed it is behind the divine idea in the mind of the Logos of our planet. In other words, it is God's will that beauty should express the strength and the reality which we call unity.

"Cultivate unity ..." You have to cultivate it. It is not ready-made, flourishing of its own nature. Man has for so long denied the existence of a Divine Plan that he has little to go on to realize that such an essential aspect of the Divine Plan as unity does not just happen by itself. It has to be cultivated and nourished. It has to be taken care of *"as a wise gardener cultivates his garden, tending carefully each new bud and shoot"*. It is not something which just grows in such a way that if you do this it will happen, and if you do not, *tant pis*, something else will happen; it is no loss. Unity has to be seen as a continuous gain, something into which you put time, energy and nourishing love, and out of that comes the beauty of the unity which can only be achieved in that way.

Likewise with every group, every nation, every grouping of nations, the same cultivation is necessary. You have to see the differences between groups, between nations, between individuals in the groups and in the nations, and seek to bridge these differences — the personality differences, the different points of view, the different emphases, the different strengths of will and purpose of the individuals — and out of that create a unity which reflects the Divine Purpose which unity itself expresses.

"Unity follows every true manifestation of love and graces each achievement of the spirit." Unity is a soul quality. It expresses the love aspect of God in its most immediate, profound and simple way. It is to do with brotherhood, with relationship. It is the achievement of right human relations. Unity is only thinkable in terms of right human relationships, and where these relationships are missing, when they are not right, then, to be sure, you do not have unity.

"Take unity as your banner and walk the way of power. Unity makes all things possible. Without unity nothing is certain; the finest possibilities come to dust." Unless you take unity as your banner, unless you follow it, raise it up and show it as your purpose, it does not happen. You have to aim at unity. You have to guard it if it is there already. For example, this group preparing the way for the reappearance of the Christ needs unity to perform that work. Without unity it could never do it. That unity is the outcome of the magnetic pull which brings the group together.

Many of you will remember, in discussing the necessary achievements for group initiation, one of the statements made was that only something like the reappearance of the Christ has a magnetic power sufficient to link together, and keep linked together, a group as various as the different groups that make up the group preparing the way for the Christ. It is a large number, but given the population of the world a tiny number of people who are doing this work. Without the inner unity built into it by the magnetic power of the idea of the return of the Christ, it could not be done; just as group initiation has always failed as an experiment on the part of the Masters Who have made many experiments with humanity, hoping to form a group who could start the work of group initiation.

The need for unity is obvious. A small number of people, 3,000 to 4,000, spread throughout the world, with the common cause of the return of the Christ and the Masters, are trying to build a resonance sufficiently loud and clear to create the climate of hope and expectancy for the return of the Christ and the Spiritual Hierarchy of Masters; and also for the externalization of the work of the Masters onto the physical plane. All of that takes unity to achieve. Anything that disturbs the unity of this union of groups of different nationalities is a threat to the basic purpose of the group, which is to prepare the way for the externalization of our Spiritual Hierarchy and to lay down the first possible steps towards group initiation.

No group has made any significant steps towards group initiation in the years in which we have discussed it, presented it as an idea. It has proved very difficult for people to understand the meaning of the requirements for group initiation, let alone actually to achieve them. From that lack of understanding, they find it impossible to focus on a discipline or a series of disciplines which will take them a little further on the road to group initiation.

Group initiation is the result of unity. That unity is linked with the power to manifest the particular achievement of group initiation. Without unity it will never take place. Perhaps it will only take place when the world as a whole achieves unity, which indeed it will do if the Masters are to be believed. They say it will.

"God's will, We affirm, will be established. Through unity and love men will come to share. Through sacrifice and reason

men will find the way to justice and peace." The Masters know that eventually the Plan will work out and these necessary achievements will take place. If they do not, then there is no hope for humanity. They have to be achieved. But just as unity does not happen by itself — it needs nourishing and looking after, consciously cultivating — so the ties that link the groups and the nations must in the same way be strengthened, nourished and cultivated to bring about the rule of law, the rule of freedom, justice and sharing in the world which alone make unity possible.

"Without unity nothing is certain; the finest possibilities come to dust. Achievement lies in the right use of the given capacities; lacking unity the highest potential may be wasted." Whatever is the potential of any man, woman, group, party or nation, it is at risk unless it has at the same time the capacity to form the correct type of ties and, therefore, to create unity between the various units who make up the groups, the parties, the nations. This is absolutely essential. Men and women of great talent, for example, become powerful politicians of all kinds, and then perhaps for lack of this spirit of unity their vision fails. Magnificent groupings, societies formed under the inspiration of an advanced initiate, which for some years flourish, bringing to the world extraordinary levels of thought from the Masters, for some reason begin to lose their focus, their power, their livingness. They end up as little more than purveyors of their own thoughtforms and their own literature handed to them by the initiate who began the group, and seeing little or no purpose in relationship to the world. They have lost not only their unity between themselves, but also the unity with their brothers and sisters in the world.

This is true for many so-called esoteric or occult organizations and societies. They have done their work in the past, failed in the past and still fail because of their inability to keep alive the basic quality of unity, and therefore livingness. If there is no unity, there is no livingness. As the Master says: *"Without such unity, it functions not as a group but blindly."* They no longer have a living purpose in their work and simply achieve the expression of already-known conditioning, and cease to move upwards and onwards.

Unity — a soul quality

"This principle can be seen at work in every branch of human activity. The rise and fall of parties, groups and even of nations are conditioned by this law." Unity is a soul quality, and is essential for the cohesion of the group. *"Too great an emphasis on individuals and personality differences thus tends to weaken the unifying ties which hold the group together."*

This reminds me of what came up in the keynote talk a couple of years ago, when the groups throughout the world were given the degree of soul and personality involvement in their work, and so could see instantly how much unity they were likely to be giving to the general unity of the group as a whole. Where the personality involvement was high and the soul aspect low, they had little to give. However active, however seemingly consistent the work, the achievement in terms of unity was relatively small. Each group throughout the world was found to have a greater or lesser degree of soul involvement, and where that was high they were obviously producing the very quality of unity which is required in the group as a whole. Where the personality involvement was high in relation to the soul involvement, then the opposite was taking place.

Groups have changed very little since then in improving the relationship between soul and personality involvement in the work. Where the soul involvement is high, it has usually been the result of the intense work of a few individuals who have reached a degree of impersonality in their work. Where impersonality exists, the ability to do the work for itself, not for any personality experience or expression or distinguishing results, then the soul aspect of that group is high. Where the personality involvement is high, the achievement of that particular group, from the Masters' point of view, is low.

These two things very clearly go together. This achievement of unity is not so easy to attain even in a group which is powerfully held together by the magnetic idea of the reappearance of the Christ. Only because of that was it thought possible, or is it even now thought possible, that this group would in any way succeed where all the other groups before it have failed in achieving the movement towards group initiation. It is so essential to maintain the unity of the group, and people do not see what hinders the nourishing of such unity.

I would say that my major task (apart from lecturing and writing) has been in upholding the group spirit, keeping up the morale of the groups. The long wait for the appearance of the Christ, for His emergence before the world, longer than I or even the Masters expected it to be by many years, has been for some people crucial. Some have learned to take themselves out of the problem, to simply do the work impersonally and achieve the kind of unity in relation to the work which they had in the beginning. Others have found it very difficult to do that. They have either left the groups or have distanced themselves from the actual work of the groups. They may have maintained a relationship to Transmission Meditation, and have come to conferences like this and have had the feeling that they were part of a unified expression of work for the reappearance of the Christ. I think a lot of that is glamour. A lot of people were deceiving themselves, and perhaps are still deceiving themselves, that their work in relation to the cause, and the importance for the world of the cause, have really matched up. With a relatively small number of people in each group, the work has gone on. People have come and gone of course. Some have become confused from a lack of certainty and have wondered if perhaps it is all a myth.

I do not know what goes on in people's minds, but if they think that maybe Maitreya is not in the world after all, that is a perfectly valid thought to occur to people. It does not, however, make sense to me in relation to the changes which are taking place in the world. One only has to look at the extraordinary changes (many predicted by Maitreya years ago) and the extraordinary miracles which take place on a daily basis, to put that one out of the window. I can understand completely people being impatient. Since Maitreya has not yet come forward I think it weakens people's resolve and morale. However, I believe Maitreya is coming forward really very soon. Going on the information which I am privileged to have, I know it to be the case. But I know that the Law does not work in the ways we would want in relation to this great event.

Until now, Maitreya has been awaiting a cycle in which there will be the best possible response from humanity to what He has to say and to give. He knows that the best possible cycle would begin with the collapse of the world's stock exchanges. That would bring humanity into reality for the first time, and it would entirely change our expectations. As long as that does not happen, the actions and expectations of the Western powers are very much at variance with the plans of Maitreya. From the point of view of the evolution of humanity, of the change of consciousness, and therefore of values which humanity needs to go forward under His banner, a crash is essential. We must *gladly* respond to His ideas: justice, freedom, and sharing for all people on Earth, not just for the Western powers. That requires a dissolution of the existing social/economic structure which so far has not occurred.

Unless Maitreya were to offend the law governing our free will, which is sacrosanct and which Hierarchy will never do, there has been little that Maitreya could do except wait and perform His miracles; and where possible impress the minds of those world leaders who are open to impression, to bring about more changes.

The reappearance of the Christ is a long time coming. However, if you have eyes to see and ears to hear, you know beyond all gainsaying that the Christ is in the world and nothing can send Him back to the Himalayas — except for a short holiday. He has been back once that I know of for three weeks. That was a long time ago.

However, to return to our theme, unity is not easily come by. We are particularly privileged in having such a powerful, motivating idea that holds the groups together. *"Unity is not too difficult to attain in the early stages of formation of a group; if the purpose of its inception is magnetic enough, that alone can hold the group together."* You cannot have an idea more powerful than that of the reappearance of the Christ and the Masters for the first time in 98,000 years. It gives us a start, and the Master would not write about unity so recently as this current issue of *Share International* if He did not mean it. There has to be a purpose behind His writing it now and in 1984.

Unity is essential but hard to achieve. The idea of the reappearance of the Christ brings the groups together in the first place. That is why there is a group several thousand strong living all over the world whose work is to make the preliminary approach to the public about it. But we have that idea so long as we believe in it. We do not have it, if we do not believe in it. Also we do not have that powerfully magnetic idea, even if we do believe in it, but have too many different ways of approaching it, too many clever ideas of making it known, too many schisms in the groups.

In the early stages everyone is filled with love, or what they take to be love — and excitement. Their astral aspiration is lifted up, they feel inspired, and it is easy to do the work. It is easy, therefore, to achieve the necessary unity which this group has shown and still shows to the world. What is difficult is to do it for ever and ever. In the case of the American groups, it has been 21 years since I first came to America and the first groups here were formed. Twenty-one years is a long time to maintain a Hierarchical idea.

All men seek unity

"Essentially, all men inwardly seek unity and find its reflection in conformity of thought and ideas. This instinct is behind the formation of political parties and other groups. The ideological consensus acts as a magnet and strengthens the potency of the whole. Groups and parties founder when the inner unity is disturbed."

It is an extraordinary thought that "all men", everyone — men, women, children — seek unity. That is what they do in their life. Have you ever thought you were seeking unity? Actually that is what you are doing. You go around looking for a group that has an idea you can relate to. It is called the reappearance of the Christ and the Masters of Wisdom. You join a group because this group is related to that idea. The very idea sparks itself in you. It is a soul idea, and your soul responds to it. That is why you joined such a group.

You do not join other groups, or some of you do. (It is a mistake but never mind!) From the point of view of the soul, you should give all your energy, all that you have that is worthwhile, to this group. That is joining. If you want unity, you cannot pick and choose. You have to give it all. (I joke, of course, but the underlying thought is important.) You may be attracted by the work of other groups but this is the only group working to prepare the way for Maitreya and His group. So leave other work to others.

192

You can expand in your sense of the group, but you cannot give a little of yourself to a group and think that you are really part of it. If you give a little of yourself, you are not being the wise gardener who is cultivating every new shoot, every new little growth. You can only pick and choose from a personality point of view. The soul does not pick and choose. It gives everything that it has. You are more of a person if you are giving your all to a cause that is bigger than yourself.

Dedication

You have to be dedicated. Dedication is a soul quality just as the nourishing, the slow building of unity, is a soul quality. The group is only functioning as a true group when it is functioning under the impulse of its soul. This is something which I think, perhaps, some people in some groups do not take in. They do not do it on a day-to-day basis. It has to be instinctive. You instinctively give all that you can to a particular cause, whichever it is. Ours happens to be the reappearance of the Christ and the return of the Masters to the everyday world, and I cannot think of anything that is so important to humanity.

Without the presence of the Masters, I believe, we would not achieve the sharing, and therefore the justice, and therefore the peace which is required. It takes the galvanizing spirit, the energy, the wisdom of the Masters to create the conditions to lift humanity, to inspire us; and also to show what will happen if we do not change. Humanity itself has to make the changes.

Long ago in the first *Agni Yoga* book, Maitreya said: *"By human hand and by human foot the New Age must be built."* Every stone, every brick, every step of the way, must be made by man himself. But it will not happen unless the Masters return to the world. It will not happen unless Maitreya not only makes Himself known but is enabled to inspire humanity to create the conditions which will lead to sharing, justice and peace. It requires the bending of every sinew, the tuning up of every nerve, to make that happen as soon as possible.

Maitreya is coming out ahead of schedule, not waiting for the stock-exchange crash: so great are the problems in the world, not least the ecological imbalance which we have created. The pollution on our planet is now the number one killer in the world. It breaks down our immune system and leaves us open to all manner of illnesses, even diseases that long ago we thought we had conquered. So it is essential that Maitreya starts His open work as soon as possible.

Also, it is essential that He does so because of the recent appointment of a new US President who is upsetting the balance of power in the world by his plans to expand, unilaterally, the national ballistic missile defence system. There is an anti-ballistic missile defence treaty which has been signed by America and Russia. It has stood the test of time and it hastened the ending of the Cold War. In the last 10 years the entire atmosphere has lightened because of the work that Maitreya has done through Mr Gorbachev in bringing this about.

Complacency

"Essentially all men inwardly seek unity and find its reflection in conformity of thought and ideas." Where the ideas conform to what you instinctively think, or where your rational mind tells you 'that is for me', you join a particular party. That is how political parties are formed. They embody certain ideas, certain ideals, and you say: "That is for me. I really go for that." Some people do not vote because they think there are no differences between the parties. But there are differences, for example, between Mr Gore and Mr Bush.

Mr Gore would not be promoting the spending of $60 billion to expand, unilaterally, the anti-ballistic missile system. It upsets the Russians. It upsets the Chinese even more. It upsets the balance of power in the world. That concerns Maitreya very seriously. In fact, He said that He will come forward sooner even than was thought possible, even before a stock exchange crash for which He has been waiting for years. The ecological and military crises that your President has provoked, and the Middle East crisis, have made it imperative that Maitreya come forward sooner than has yet seemed possible. I think the movement outwards by Maitreya would promote a stock-exchange crash. This would bring humanity to its senses in the quickest possible way, seeing reality as it is for the first time.

In America you really have no idea what it is like even in the poorer parts of Eastern Europe, let alone in the developing world, in India or Africa. Africa is a case all on its own. The depth of misery is so extraordinary there that people in this country cannot even begin to believe it. Your media do not help because they have withdrawn from almost all the media outlets any sign of developing-world misery and poverty. There are few media programmes that bring it to mind: for the most part they see that that kind of media concern is bad for business. If you look at it, you will switch stations. And if you switch stations you will not watch the commercials. If you do not watch the commercials, you will not buy the products. So they make sure that you do not see the misery by omitting to put it on the screens.

Interconnectedness of all atoms

"The underlying purpose of all life is the creation of unity, thus expressing the interconnectedness of all atoms." This is the most extraordinary statement, I think, made by my Master. Maitreya has also stated, as a fact of life, that all atoms are connected. We are part of that matter and of all atoms throughout cosmos. That interconnectedness, that lack of separation anywhere, makes it real, makes it manifest in your

mind, that if you see yourself as a soul, if you see the world as the soul sees the world, that is how it is. You see the world where every particle is interconnected.

Every soul is a part of one soul. There is no such thing as a separate soul. Each soul is an individualized fragment of one great oversoul, and that oversoul in its turn is part of all that exists in spirit in the world. And that is all that exists. All of that is differentiated into the myriad forms which we see, including ourselves. We see ourselves as the human form, tall or short, fat or thin. There are myriad forms throughout cosmos and every one of them, including all the human beings, are interrelated in the sense that they are all atoms. There is only the atomic structure of all cosmos. That is where we come from. That is, as the Master says, "the Source of our Being".

"For most men, cosmos is a collection of separate material bodies, infinitely large and distant ..." There is Mars. There is star number XYZ out there. There is a nebula out there. They are so vast, so far away. They seem to have nothing to do with us. But they have. The atomic structure which makes them up is the same atomic structure which makes up our bodies, the same atomic structure in everything we see and everything we can visualize in the universe. In reality: *"Space Itself is a living entity, the Source of our Being, our Mother and Father. As souls, we know this to be so, and seek to give expression to the fundamental unity of our nature."* We seek to find the soul's awareness of the unity of all life where we can. We find it in groups. We find it to some extent in political parties. We find it in nations. This is why people identify with their nations. This is why, if you are American, you identify with America. If you are Russian, you identify with Russia, and so on. That is why, if you have a broader view, you identify not only with your nation but with the community of nations. You see all the nations as one.

It is not good if only 180 nations sign the Kyoto Agreement. Your nation (the US) is only 5 per cent of the world's population, so it is not essential, you might say. However, it *is* essential because it causes 25 per cent of all the pollution in the world. Yet your government refuses to sign the Kyoto Agreement, which 180 nations have signed. It does not mean they are actually doing the work — they are only agreeing to limit for a time the exuding of gases. There is much more they have to do, but it is a step forward. Your government, your President, has refused to sign. In fact, he says: "It is against American interest to do it." You have to be allowed to send up more of these gases.

This is the key to the whole thing: everyone looks to identify with something larger than themselves. That sense of unity is essential because everyone is looking for it whether they know they are looking for it or not. Unity is the soul's awareness of the unity of cosmos. Nothing less than that. And where you create unity in your work, in your group, in your nation, or in the group of nations, you benefit humanity.

"A group, therefore, loses this unity at its peril." Whatever weakens the unity of a group is perilous for the group. *"Without such unity it functions not as a group but blindly, without purpose and cohesion, a disparate collection of attitudes and conditioning."* So let nothing influence you towards the weakening of the group's unity. It is essential to the very nature of the group as it exists, to the work that the group is doing, and to any future work that the group is asked to do.

Luckily, we are entering the Age of Aquarius. The quality of the energy of Aquarius is Synthesis. Synthesis takes disparate, varied attitudes and fuses and blends them into one. It creates out of that variety a unity. The creation of unity, according to the Master, is the aim of all life. That is the underlying purpose of our lives. Therefore, you can see how important it is that

197

unity should be fostered and nourished in every possible way. Everything that denies it, qualifies it, reduces it, weakens it, is against the life of the group, against the life of the planet if you consider it in international terms. It is absolutely essential that the American people join with all the other people of the world to set to rights the ecology of the world. There is no way you can get out of it. There is no way you can wait. You have to force your government to see that this is bigger than America.

America is only 5 per cent of the world's population, so it is easy for everything to be bigger than America. It is 3,000 miles across, maybe 1,000 miles north to south. It feels like the world. The world begins in New York and finishes in San Francisco. This being so, it is very easy, if you are American, to feel that not only is it the biggest, and militarily the most powerful, country in the world, it is also the most important in the world. But it is not the most important in the world. From the economic point of view today it is the richest country in the world. But how long is that going to last? As soon as the stock exchange crashes, the people who consider themselves rich will be poor.

That which brought down Rome, and brought down every ancient civilization, is here in America. It is the same situation. You have run it for too long, and too far. You turn greedy and selfish and power-hungry. When men do that, they go down. No nation can work against the plan of evolution for ever. For a little time, yes, until it waxes strong and powerful, rich militarily and economically. But the rest of the world is growing too. It may be groaning, but it is groaning and growing. It grows in its demands. The rest of the world is now growing in its demands on the developed world — not only America, but Europe and Japan and the developed world generally.

These demands must be met. We cannot create the New Age built on justice and sharing if we do not. It is not possible, we cannot have it both ways. That is why the Masters are returning to the world now rather than later, because time is short. The crisis is too great for Them to leave it too long. Then we would have gone over the edge. So we must create unity in an international sense. Individually we cannot do it, but together we can. *"Together, men can perform all manner of mighty deeds. Limitless are the possibilities of change, but men must act together to create the new world. Through unity alone will men conquer. The strength of unity will open all gates. Hold fast to the ideal of brotherhood and cease to mock your brother's efforts. Know that he, too, faces the storm and struggles in the dark."*

That is what we are all doing. We are out in little boats in the storm, in the dark. We cannot see the stars, we see nothing to guide us. We are rowing against the tide or with the tide, and looking up for a light to guide us. That new light, the light to guide us, is the Christ, if men did but know it. The light of His love and wisdom; the light of His vision of the future; the light of His nearness to the Source of Light and Life Itself. He is here, ready to guide humanity out of the quicksands, out of the torrents, out of the storms which otherwise prevail. In this way, He will set His seal on this time, the time of the return to the world of the Wise Men of the world, the Inspirers, the Guides.

As the Master has put it: *"The first step is to accept that all is One. Underlying the diversity of forms beats the heart of the One Divine Life. When mankind grasps this truth, there will emerge a civilization based upon that truth which will carry man to the feet of Divinity Itself. Then the gateway to the heavens will open and man will find himself on a journey without end. The cosmos near and far will be the subject of his research. Infinity will beckon him ever onwards and test his valour."* ('The Divine science' by the Master —, through Benjamin Creme, *Share International* March 1986)

We are now making little experiments and touching the planets, taking photographs. In a very short time we will explore all the planets of our system in spaceships. Maybe not this generation, but not so far ahead. And in time we will go to the furthest extent of our galaxy.

When man sees the universe and himself as One, all things become possible. We have to see ourselves as One and at one with the universe: that there is no difference between us and the universe; that we are intrinsically related to every other being on Earth and everything on Earth; that the atomic structure which makes us up, makes up everything we can see in the whole of cosmos; that there is only unity.

Therefore, this longing for unity, this joining of groups, this growingness of groups, and in this new age of Aquarius this group endeavour, will become *the* endeavour. Nothing of any great import will be attempted on an individual basis. It is the age of the group, expanding the activity until the whole world is working together, expressing the basic unity of planet Earth.

"Man will come to sense himself as an integral unit in a vast system that stretches to the stars. As a tiny point of conscious, loving life without which the universe would be poorer." (ibid.)

Reference: *Agni Yoga Series* (various works). Agni Yoga Society, New York.

UNITY — THE AIM OF LIFE

QUESTIONS AND ANSWERS

[Questions without publication date are from the 2001 conferences in the USA and the Netherlands and were published in **Share International**, *January/February 2002.]*

Unity in Diversity

The idea of unity can seem boring. How does this thought affect the desire for unity in a group situation?

The idea that unity should seem boring is to me an appalling thought. I do not see how it could enter anyone's mind who has understood what we are talking about. The aim of our life, whether we have realized it or not, is the establishment of unity, representing the unity which already exists because every atom in the manifested universe is interrelated with every other atom.

Unity is not simply an idea which we can hold or not hold; it is driving us on our evolutionary process. This evolution, expansion of consciousness, must be a process of ever-widening awareness of unity and a synthesis of all the possible aspects of unity that exist until you have the 'Mind of God', seeing the unity that underlies the whole of existence.

How that could be boring puzzles me; it shows a tremendous difference in approach to the word unity. It seems that some of the people in the group see unity as a stereotyped experience, everyone thinking in the same way, every reaction, every approach the same. If that were unity, of course it would become boring. But that is not what we are talking about. We are talking about the fundamental basis of our existence. If it is true that unity is basic to our existence, born out of the identity of all atoms with all other atoms, then unity is, perhaps, very different from what you think.

My own idea of unity is of the utmost possible diversity. As you know, there are seven rays of energy, and these in their various relationships produce all the phenomena that we see and experience. Because of that there is infinite diversity. All the nations share these seven rays as souls and as personalities. In this way nations are very varied in their qualities.

My understanding of the Master's articles on 'Unity' and 'The need for unity' is that they are not only to do with group work; although He does relate them to the workings of groups, He also relates them to the world scene. He is really talking about international relationships and the need for unity in that area; that is the urgency. Your own group relationships need the understanding and growth of unity, but they do not have the same effect on the world as, for example, Mr Bush's lack of a sense of the unity necessary to produce co-operation and so solve the problems of the world. Only unity can work co-operatively.

We know that the most efficient exponents of competition, the opposite of co-operation, have been America, the various countries of Europe, Japan, Australia and Canada. A very limited number of countries are, in fact, 'running the show'. The world is much too complex. Therefore, the problems involved in its development, even maintaining its physical existence, demand co-operation and peace, the ability to work together to solve problems which are threatening the very existence of the world. These are the real problems that the Master is talking about in these articles on unity.

He relates the articles to the groups because He has various groups under His charge, and He is developing the two things —

the ideas in relation to both the groups and the international scene — because the groups relate to the world. The effects on the groups are relatively unimportant compared with the effects that unity or competition have on the world, on our international relations. If, for example, America had signed the Kyoto Protocol for the stabilization of greenhouse-gas emissions, it would have been a good idea not only because 180 nations saw it as a good idea — and, I have no doubt, many Americans did too — but because Mr Bush stands for a certain approach. He stands for a Republican approach to that problem. Historically this has been whatever is seen as being in the best interest of the country they represent, the United States. The representatives of every country at any given time are no doubt looking after the most crucial interests of their nation as they see it. Some nations are a little more advanced, have a little more soul involvement in their consciousness, and so look on a broader scale. They are able to see not only their own personal interests but can take a wider view from time to time, and that is good and useful. So it depends on the point of evolution reached, and on the importance of the idea or problem.

I would say that diversity is the fundamental nature of the life of humanity. The individuality of every human being is not only a fact; it is one of the great facts of human evolution. Individuality shows the uniqueness of every person. As an extension of the individual, every nation is a soul with a personality. Either the personality ray, or the soul ray, is uppermost, more influential.

Unfortunately, at the present time, the soul ray is hidden for the most part by the activity of the lesser ray, the personality ray, and most nations just look after their own personal interests so far as they can. If they are big, powerful nations like the United States or the Europeans, they do it more effectively than small nations who do not have the clout, internationally, to make their voices heard or have any effect on the whole.

The greatest diversity within the greatest unity, or put the other way, the greatest unity with the greatest diversity, is the ideal which humanity is seeking, and is in alignment with the Plan of our Logos for the development of this world. It is not a boring sameness — in fact, the very opposite. Maitreya in one of His early messages [No.3] said: "*Let Me take you by the hand and take you into a land where no man lacks, where no two days are alike, where the joy of brotherhood manifests through all men.*"

"*Where no two days are alike*" is, to me, an extraordinary statement. The only people for whom no two days are alike are young children and the rare person who has enough money and leisure to do what he wants to do, in which he can fill his life creatively, moment to moment, so that there is no drudgery. Boredom and drudgery come out of sameness. In unity there is no sameness. It is not about the repetition of like ideas time and again until it gets boring. It is creatively seeing life and, therefore, every aspect, every movement, of that life creatively, newly, moment to moment. When you are in the state of unity that the Master is talking about, that is the state of timeless, creative existence which exists for us all.

Consensus

How much conflict can we tolerate in the group without it threatening the unity of the group?

The short answer to that is none. Every manifestation of conflict threatens the unity of the group. By the same token, unity is not possible for groups who cannot create a consensus. If you can create a consensus, conflict does not arise. However, few groups can create an ongoing consensus and so you have conflict arising many times. How much does that affect the unity of the group? It depends on the severity of the conflict. If it is very severe it could threaten the very existence of the group.

It is not a group if it does not have a degree — though not necessarily a perfected degree — of unity, because unity is the very nature of a group. You cannot take away the unity and still have the group. It is something else then: people with a set of different ideas, who air their conditioned ideas, their personal prejudices. That has nothing to do with the synthesis, the consensus of thought, which is essentially a group expression. This comes out of the nature of the group action.

This idea of a consensus has been brought up before. There are those who think that there is no such thing as consensus, that it does not actually exist. You just 'play your corner' and you win some ideas and proposals and you lose others; that is all that there is. That is not true. That is a deeply materialistic, and to my mind, wrong view of what thought is, what ideas are. Every idea that comes to us is in some way, perhaps only tenuously, to do with real life. If it is even somewhat to do with real life, it has to reflect reality. The reality in some situations, not group situations, is that you put out your ideas; you win some and you lose some. It is a businessman's approach. You win some sales and you lose other sales.

That is the materialistic view of life. It does not concern us. It is not relevant to the idea of unity, or how much conflict a unified group can sustain. That depends on the intensity of the conflict. If it is a minor conflict the unity of the group will usually rise above it. If it is longstanding, and there are some groups in which there is longstanding conflict, it is like a drop of water dripping on a stone, eating away at the unity of the stone until it has created a hole.

The same thing happens in a group. Minor conflicts are easy to resolve with goodwill and co-operation. Co-operation is an absolute essential for the creation of unity because it is an aspect of unity. If you have a unified view of the universe, of the problems of the world, you recognize that they involve everybody. Everybody in the world is affected by the big problems like pollution, global warming, the rising of the seas, and so on. These problems have to be tackled through co-operation. There is no other way. No one can say that it does not concern them. Life on earth is threatened. I do not mean just by terrorists. Terrorism is an effect. To understand it you have to look for the cause which relates to those who have and those who have not, to those who have power and those who resent, or want a share in, that power. It is not the cause of disunity, but an effect of the *malaise* which is already there. It expresses itself among certain individuals as terrorism, as the most effective, cheapest, and, if you are a fanatic, natural way to show your readiness to die for an idea. People have long been dying for ideas. It is the extreme sacrifice which is presented to the world by the Piscean experience. As long as the energy of Pisces is producing the effects of exclusion and division, that possibility will go on.

If you have no consensus in your group you will have disunity. If you cannot even accept the existence of consensus as an idea, you will never have unity.

How can we come to a consensus? (January/February 1998)

There is only one way to come to a consensus: co-operation. As soon as you co-operate, consensus becomes possible. While you have competition in presentation of points of view, you get no consensus, because everyone wants their point of view to be taken up and made the general view. Then it becomes a majority, which has nothing to do with consensus. Consensus is the intuitive, and therefore soul, understanding that a certain process, realized and acted on by a group, is the one and only action for that time and place. In this way consensus becomes a very dynamic force. As soon as you have true consensus you have the entire energy — the will, love and intelligence — of the group as a whole behind it. It is as if something new, a synthetic voice, has been created, that brings together all the disparate points of view, all the different nuances, reservations. All of these suddenly coalesce in an intuitive way in the group that is working in total co-operation. The end view is known, accepted and realized in the same way by everyone, and consensus suddenly descends into the group with all the energy of the soul behind it.

The action coming from consensus does the work. That should be the aim of all the actions of the group: to make them so fused and blended together that they produce, as it were, a rod of steel, hard and sharp, which goes straight to carry out its task. Otherwise it is a question of trying a little bit here and a little bit there. It is diffused, and therefore relatively ineffective.

From time to time a kind of inspiration acts as the synthesizing fire which brings about a red-hot, natural action which goes straight to the target. You can recognize it when you see it. You cannot think it up; it simply happens when the group co-operates to such a degree that their minds and intuition fuse together in an action which is self-evidently the natural, best way to proceed. This leaves out the entire question of criticism or questioning. The action itself becomes a crucible in which all the ideas, the intent, the intelligence and creative ability of the group fuse together. That is a group thought, a group action, and nothing can compare with it.

Priority

Sometimes it seems a lot of energy can be expended in trying to achieve group unity and cohesion, often to no avail. Which is the group priority — creating unity or getting the word out?

The work of the groups is to get the word out about the reappearance. In doing that you either work as a group or you do not. If you work as a group then group unity becomes a factor.

This group is different in that it is working for the reappearance, but it is also working to achieve the beginning of group initiation. That is ongoing and it takes time. The reappearance work has an end time: Maitreya will come out, people will see Him. That particular aspect of the work is nearing its close. The ongoing work of group initiation will, or should, engage the attention of all groups everywhere because that is basic to what we are doing.

Hierarchy never does one thing at a time. With every expenditure of energy They do two or three or four things that are going forward simultaneously. They have found a group, brought them into incarnation and given them this huge, magnetic idea of the reappearance of the Christ, which is powerful enough to link together these disparate groups, all activated by the same cause.

As I have said before, some groups are more 'together' than others. In some groups 90 per cent of their activity is soul directed. There are other groups where only 30 per cent of their action is soul directed, which means that 70 per cent of their action is directed from the brain, from the personality level. That makes a difference in the quality of the group, in the tone, the note sounded occultly. The Masters see every group in terms of the note which is struck, the degree of soul integration.

Some groups, therefore, manifest more of the soul energy and others more of the personality energy at this time. They have room to grow, but that is how it is at the moment. Those in which the soul is more involved have fewer problems of the kind mentioned. Those where the personality is more to the fore have more of these problems. We have to accept it. They have to go through it and develop soul direction and infuse the work of their group with the soul. All, more or less, are doing their best.

Trust

What is the major factor preventing unity in the groups?

The major factor preventing unity in the groups is criticism, which the Master mentioned in the first article. Criticism of individuals by one or more members is very destructive of group unity.

Criticism, however, is of two kinds, constructive and destructive. It is usually destructive but it need not be. There is positive, constructive criticism. For example, a Master or an enlightened teacher who points out to a disciple or an aspirant his or her faults, bad habits or destructive tendencies, is being constructive about a destructive attitude. The person may be quite unaware of the destructiveness of his or her criticism, for instance, and think that they are only pointing out the obvious. But to the person concerned, the obvious might be not at all clear. They might be totally unaware of what, to the criticizer, seems obvious to everyone.

Usually we criticize what we dislike in ourselves. We project that onto others whom we do not like too much. In so doing we are getting rid of it for the time being, putting it on to somebody else and criticizing them for having that particular fault, glamour or form of behaviour which we may have all the time. That is very destructive. It destroys group unity because it destroys the trust between the members of the group.

This is why, in the economic field, it is so important to introduce the process of sharing first of all, before anything else. Every problem of the world will need sharing for its own resolution. Sharing by its very nature creates trust because it is an expression of the Love aspect of God. It is in everybody, but in many people it is covered up, hidden, never shown the light of day. Some people are absolutely against sharing the resources of the developed world with the developing world. They think there is no reason why they should give away, as they see it, their hard-won wealth to those 'long-haired-weirdoes' who are work-shy, do nothing, and have no jobs (because there are no jobs for them to have). This is very difficult to cut through.

There is a huge body of opinion in the United States that considers what you make in life (and there is strength in it, too), is a better gain to you, a better proof of your reality, your individuality, your being as a man or woman, than a state which provides goods so that nobody goes hungry. They do not see that if the state does not do so, those people do not eat. If they do not eat, they die. They do not look at the simple truth that if you do not eat enough, you die of starvation. Millions do not eat enough to keep alive. Somehow these people can say: "Well, it is no fault of mine, and it is no concern of mine."

In America the idea of being in a wilderness which is still being opened up is quite strong even though they may be the fourth or fifth generation to be living in luxury in the sun in California. They are dealing with high technological industry which is very far from the early settlers who came in caravans and lived in log cabins a century and a half ago.

The people with this particular view have the feeling that they are pioneers still. You have everything to win or to lose, it is up to you. It is not up to the state, or a town council, or the sheriff. It is up to you as a man with a spade or a gun to make out of life what you can. It is a pioneer spirit, which has a terrific vitality and is expressed today at its best in the tremendous energy which radiates through the United States. It is, at its best, all that is best in America. But it also has this narrow view that you get nothing for nothing in this life. Yet the same people invest in the stock market because there they do get something for nothing. They are not very consistent.

When you share, you create trust because you have expressed love. Sharing is the expression of love. In a family they share all the resources according to the needs of the family. The sense of being one family is very much overdue in this world. By sharing you create the trust which allows you to trust other people. If you show trust, you receive trust. By sharing what you have with others, it creates that trust without which no major decisions will ever be made. Without trust there will never be a consensus on the overriding problems which concern this world, which can only be met internationally. In fact, Maitreya has said that everybody — every man, woman and child — must see the upholding of the planet itself as the number one priority in the world. All must take part. You may smile at the idea of children doing it but if there is a campaign for recycling, in any town, children are the first to get their parents to do it. They go out there and organize the recycling. Recycling is just one of the many ways in which the goods of the earth can be preserved for generations to come.

When you have trust you can do anything. The major reason for conflict in groups is criticism, because criticism affects the trust. Just as you can change the world through sharing, and create trust, without trust in a group you cannot have unity. It is impossible. Criticism breaks down the trust, and therefore the unity.

"To silence the tongues of criticism." Does that also mean to silence the thought?

Yes, of course. The 'tongues' are the result of the thought. You have to think before you speak. The "tongues of criticism" is a good phrase, and we know what the Master means. He means also the thoughts. Destructive thinking that is not voiced is just as harmful to the person who thinks it, to the person receiving it, and to the group as a whole, as if it is voiced, because the person behaves as he or she would do if they were going to say it. They are meaning it all the time.

Discrimination

You said there were too many clever ideas. What do you mean?

There are clever ideas and there are creative clever ideas. An idea that is creative will be clever; it will be new. Anything creative has in it something of the new. That is what makes it doubtful to some people. Anything new makes people doubt its veracity or its quality, but you have to use your common sense. By too many clever ideas I meant too many gimmicks, sales gimmicks, as it were, used in commercial advertising. Usually, these are inappropriate for our use.

When does a creative idea become too clever, that is, harmful for group unity?

If it is a creative idea, I do not think it becomes harmful for group unity. If it is a truly creative idea, it is probably self-evidently beneficial for the group and so is not against group unity. If it is tremendously creative and clever perhaps the group as a whole does not understand it, and it does not get implemented. But it should not be harmful to group unity.

The worst ideas are the destructive ones. Any ideas that are basically not true are harmful for the group. An idea that is not true, but which is accepted by some as true, is destructive of the unity of the group because some people will believe it and others will reject it. Some will say: "It is true. It feels true to me." Others will say: "I do not believe that. It does not feel true to me. It has the smell of glamour."

The trouble with glamour is that it is highly infectious. It is like an infectious disease which can go through the whole group, and the group may be broken up because of it. When the glamour has to do with ideas which are false, it is very destructive of group unity because some will take them as true. Their glamour accommodates itself to the glamour of the untruth, and they do not see anything wrong with it. Others who have more discrimination can see immediately from the discriminating faculty of the mind, which is the soul through the mind, that it is glamour, untrue and they do not want anything to do with it. And so you get disunity in the group. That is one of the most powerful destructive agencies in a group.

How do we deal with this kind of situation without getting into criticism? How do we deal with that particular kind of glamour?

If you think that something is basically untrue, you are not talking about a different approach, a purely personality difference because of ray-structure, training or habit. People will have all sorts of different ideas of how certain activities should be done. Most squabbles in groups are on that level. But it may be a question of: "Is what we are putting out actually true or not? Is it simply a glamour, a false idea of a particular individual who some people think is telling the truth?" Maybe that person thinks he is telling the truth, but the others from their point of discrimination say it is not true. Then you have to say: "For me this is glamour. For me this is not true. I cannot go forward on that premise."

For myself, throughout the last 27 years of releasing the information about the return of the Christ and Hierarchy, there has been one factor which I have kept solid and above all: that what I say I believe from my *experience* to be true. I cannot say what I do not believe to be true. I cannot say it with conviction, so there is no point in saying it at all. When what you say is true

213

in itself and you say it with the conviction which personal experience gives you, you are believed. If it is true, it has a power which only truth itself has. If it is glamour, false, an illusion of truth, it does not have that power. It may last for a fortnight or six months or a year, but then it will disappear as if it had never been. By all media rules, this information should have been as dead as the dodo long ago, and yet this is not the case. In fact, it is now believed more readily than ever before.

So it is better not to act on the glamour?

Those who do not believe the glamour must not act on it as if it were true. Those who believe that a certain thing is true could be wrong or could be right, but they believe it, and they act on that. Time will tell which is the truth and which is the glamour. Most people are glamoured. They are at a level in their evolution in which the astral plane is their focus of consciousness. That is their area of sensitivity for any ideas to be registered and assessed. So they cannot do other than be glamoured to a greater or lesser extent.

The process of becoming a disciple is an achieving of discrimination, so that instantly you know if something has the feel of truth. Your own soul through the mind tells you it is true or tells you that it is false. This is the most divisive thing in a group because there will be some who do not have that discriminating faculty, and so cannot make up their mind about it. They do not know. They want somebody to tell them what is true and what is not. Anyone who talks a lot or writes books, like me, tends to be believed because they talk a lot and write books. It does not necessarily make your statements true. What reveals your truth is your discrimination and the conviction with which you speak.

You can ask if these ideas match up with the esoteric information, going back to the *Upanishads* if necessary, through the *Bhagavad Gita,* through all the teachings given to the world up to Jesus and the Koran. Does it match up to Blavatsky and Alice Bailey? Is there a connecting link with all of that, or is there some huge discrepancy?

If it is true, it will be true to the nature of life. When it is false, it is against the nature of life. People love glamour. Ninety-plus per cent of the world are glamoured because that is the level at which they are living. Essentially, the astral plane is unreal, but for most people it is real. Therefore, it has a glamourous appeal. It fills the astral bookshops of the world. It is an entry for a lot of people into something higher but that does not mean *it* is higher. It just means it is an *entry* to something higher.

Are people 'improving' at all, getting free of glamour?

I am conscious from my lectures and radio or television interviews that the questions are a bit more real, they are somewhat less glamoured, although there is plenty of that, too. It is the same thing as in false religious teachings: it is conditioning. In a sense glamour is conditioning. It is the conditioned mind that looks for a quick and easy or magical answer to the problems of the world. There are no quick and easy answers to deep human problems, problems of the growth of consciousness. You do not need a man from the other side of the galaxy to come and put his hand on your head and remove your blindness and glamour, and suddenly you see all as it is in the mind of God. That sounds nice in a book but it is nonsense. Nobody is going to come from the other side of the galaxy to do that to somebody who has not yet taken even the first initiation. No one is going to come from the other side of the galaxy at all. You have to put things in perspective. The trouble is that people cannot do that. They do not have the faculty of discrimination to do that, so they can believe anything. When you believe *anything* you get into trouble.

But the glamoured person can also be speaking with conviction because they would not know that they were glamoured.

Precisely. The person who is putting out the glamoured information may believe in it completely because they are so englamoured that they do not know the difference. It comes to them on the astral plane and it is like dreams. You go to sleep and you dream. If your dreams were reality, you could do anything. You can think of anything in your dream, and it is there. Likewise on the astral plane. Whatever you want, whatever you think of, is there, and you can visualize anything you want: Masters meeting you, dozens of Them, on some high plain in the Himalayas or the Andes. You are shaking hands with each one and They are bowing to you. Then you realize what you never did before, how august, how great, how evolved you really are. And nobody noticed it, nobody came up to you and said: "You know, you are right. We always felt that about you. You are different." Glamour is a minefield.

People are so immersed in themselves that they believe everything that they experience, including their astral dreams when they are awake. They believe it and think it is real, just as you think for a few seconds that your dream is real. You come out of the dream and say: "Ah, it was only a dream, what a shame," or: "Thank God, it was only a dream." Most times you are too busy looking and thinking and doing to pay attention to these astral imaginings. In some people these are so much with them that they get all sorts of intimations and they say: "I have a feeling; I feel that this is so." If you are a disciple and you know something, you do not feel it, you know it. You know it or you do not know it, you never feel it. Astrally-focused people always feel it. "I have a feeling that this is happening or this is going to happen." You can be sure that it is not, because it is just a feeling like any other dream.

When certain information is presented from different publishers and other sources, maybe we are able to see that some information is very glamoured, but in this country when it is endorsed and published by the co-ordinating centre, then that conditions peoples' minds as to whether it is true or not.

Absolutely. People look for security in what they read. They cannot read everything, and they want to read what is valuable. What is valuable is what feels good, is interesting, satisfying, what feeds their glamours, their mind, their imagination, or gives them a new view of life. In most cases publishers stick to one kind of literature, and you know what that publisher's book is going to be like — very glamoured indeed and speaking to the least evolved of the reading public. Then there are those who have more discrimination, and they go up a notch. Maybe stuff coming from the sixth rather than the fifth astral plane. Most of the really glamoured stuff — the meat-and-drink glamour — comes from the fifth astral plane.

The sixth astral plane is where you get higher aspirational teaching. For example, *A Course in Miracles* was given by the Master Jesus to a disciple who works on the sixth astral plane. That disciple gave it to a medium (although she did not know she was a medium) who took it down. It is pretty pure. That is an example of a very high level of teaching coming from one of the Masters, which eventually reached the physical plane but from the sixth astral plane.

This is a way in which quite high spiritual teaching can be given on the astral planes. Normally, the Masters eschew the astral planes. They never work on the fifth astral plane Themselves, but They do give work, or experiences, from time to time, on the sixth astral, the plane which is more to do with

217

the heart than the solar plexus. At the higher levels of the sixth astral, it is relatively pure. It is all relative. The aspiration of the individual can allow it to be given, if that is where they are sensitive.

The Masters would no doubt love all disciples to be sensitive on the highest soul plane, but this is not the case. They would love it even if they were all sensitive on the mental plane. This, too, is not the case. So if They want to give out information, if They want to reach as many people as possible, the Masters from time to time spread the net a bit wider. It has problems connected with it, but They use people from time to time who are astral sensitives, and who can only receive on the astral plane. If it can be the sixth astral plane, so much the better. They sometimes give experiences there. That is why so many people have come to the world's attention as 'Maitreya' or 'the Christ'. All these people are responding to the Hierarchical idea that the Christ is returning to the world, but they think it is themselves.

[Editor's note – There are seven levels in the astral plane, the seventh being the highest of the astral planes. Above the astral plane, there are four levels of mental plane, the fourth being the highest. Above the mental plane exists the soul plane, the spiritual plane.]

Group Unity

Our group discussed the different means we all use to get the word out. That is, getting the Emergence news out, using various local speakers, and lately using national speakers because they attract more people. Can you talk about how these or various other things contribute to or detract from our group purpose?

If they are all getting the word out, and it is the same word, and the word is true, there is no difference. There is no harm being done. If, on the other hand, untruths are given out, that is a different matter altogether. When people put out untruths it is destructive and harmful to the cause, harmful to the group as a group, and harmful to Maitreya and to the Plan.

The Masters do not look for perfection. If They did there would be nothing done because there is no perfection anywhere. They even accept some of the most glamoured individuals I have ever come upon as being useful in their way; information stemming from sources that to me are 100 per cent from the fifth astral plane. They accept that as useful in that it brings the *idea* of the Masters to the world. These people may be absolutely wrong about the Masters: Who the Masters are, what Their function is, how They work. There are all sorts of different 'teachings' about Masters.

If people are giving out information about the return of the Christ and the Masters to the world, it behoves us to be as accurate as we possibly can.

If unity did not underlie all life then the dark forces would not seek to collect converts to their cause but would be content to live in isolation. Their not knowing this is their weakness. Our not knowing this is their strength.

That would be true if it were true. Certainly our not knowing that is their strength, but they do know that unity underlies the whole of life. They see themselves as the exponents of this unity. They are at war with the Forces of Light; they have no love in their nature. They have enthralled humanity for more than 98,000 years and seek to go on enthralling humanity. But they will not continue to do so.

They know without a shadow of a doubt that when Maitreya and the Masters appear openly in the world their control is in peril. They will be sealed off to their own domain, which is simply upholding the matter aspect of the planet. There it is not evil but normal; that is their role. Their influence vis-à-vis humanity will gradually end.

Does a demonstration of harmlessness include the use of force and even anger?

It does not include the use of force but it may include not the use of anger but the appearance of anger. Masters have been known to shout at the tops of Their voices in an apparently angry outburst which, of course, is fictitious. It is simply a colouring that They may add to bring attention to what They have to say, and to make a criticism when necessary.

Does the continued existence of regular group meetings foster group unity, or are they a dissipation of group energy?

You could have group meetings every day of the week and this could foster group unity, or you could have group meetings every day of the week and it could do the very opposite; it could just dissipate group energy. It depends on what you do at the meeting, how you act, how detached are the individuals in the group. How obsessed are they with their own ideas, or otherwise? Obsession with an idea which runs counter to that of all the other members of the group is usually a glamour and very dissipating of group energy.

To what extent does the use of mantras, particularly The Mantram of Unification, help to cause group unity?

There are mantras and mantras. If we all went around saying "*OM Mani Padme Hum*", I do not think it would do much for group unity. But if you use 'The Mantram of Unification'* on a daily basis, it does not solve all the problems of the world, but it will tend to keep your mind focused on the need for unity. It was given by the Master Djwhal Khul through Alice Bailey. It is quite long, but you can memorize and say it daily, as many times a day as you like, and it focuses your mind on the idea of unity, the oneness of all humanity. It is very beautiful, and very worthwhile learning and using.

* See Alice A.Bailey, *The Externalisation of the Hierarchy.* Lucis Press, London, 1957, p142.

Take My hand, My friends, and let Me lead you over the river.
Let Me guide you over the narrow bridge.

Let Me show you the beauty which rests on the other side.
That beauty, My friends, is your true Self.

Help Me, My friends, to help you, and together let us transform this world.

From Message No. 130 — 20 October 1981

TRANSMISSION MEDITATION

— A BRIEF EXPLANATION —

A group meditation providing both a dynamic service to the world and powerful, personal spiritual development.

Transmission Meditation is a group meditation established to better distribute spiritual energies from their custodians, the Masters of Wisdom, our planetary Spiritual Hierarchy. It is a means of "stepping down" (transforming) these energies so that they become accessible and useful to the general public. It is the creation, in co-operation with the Hierarchy of Masters, of a vortex or pool of higher energy for the benefit of humanity.

In March 1974, under the direction of his Master, Benjamin Creme formed the first Transmission Meditation group in London. Today there are hundreds of Transmission Meditation groups around the world and new groups are forming all the time.

Transmission Meditation groups provide a link whereby Hierarchy can respond to world need. The prime motive of this work is service, but it also constitutes a powerful mode of personal growth. Many people are searching for ways in which to improve the world — this desire to serve can be strong, but difficult, in our busy lives, to fulfil. Our soul needs a means to serve, but we do not always respond to its call, and so produce disequilibrium and conflict within ourselves. Transmission Meditation provides a unique opportunity for service in a potent and fully scientific way with the minimum expenditure of one's time and energy.

Benjamin Creme holds Transmission Meditation workshops around the world. During the meditation he is overshadowed by

Benjamin Creme holds Transmission Meditation workshops around the world. During the meditation he is overshadowed by Maitreya, the World Teacher, which allows Maitreya to confer great spiritual nourishment on the participants. Many people are inspired to begin Transmission Meditation after attending such a workshop, and many acknowledge having received healing in the process.

[Please refer to *Transmission: A Meditation for the New Age* by Benjamin Creme.]

THE PRAYER FOR THE NEW AGE

I am the creator of the universe.

I am the father and mother of the universe.

Everything came from me.

Everything shall return to me.

Mind, spirit and body are my temples,

For the Self to realize in them

My supreme Being and Becoming.

The Prayer for the New Age, given by Maitreya, the World Teacher, is a great mantram or affirmation with an invocative effect. It will be a powerful tool in the recognition by us that man and God are One, that there is no separation. The 'I' is the Divine Principle behind all creation. The Self emanates from, and is identical to, the Divine Principle.

The most effective way to use this mantram is to say or think the words with focused will, while holding the attention at the ajna centre between the eyebrows. When the mind grasps the meaning of the concepts, and simultaneously the will is brought to bear, those concepts will be activated and the mantram will work. If it is said seriously every day, there will grow inside you a realization of your true Self.

THE GREAT INVOCATION

From the point of Light within the Mind of God
Let light stream forth into the minds of men.
Let Light descend on Earth.

From the point of Love within the Heart of God
Let love stream forth into the hearts of men.
May Christ return to Earth.

From the centre where the Will of God is known
Let purpose guide the little wills of men —
The Purpose which the Masters know and serve.

From the centre which we call the race of men
Let the Plan of Love and Light work out
And may it seal the door where evil dwells.

Let Light and Love and Power
Restore the Plan on Earth.

The Great Invocation, used by the Christ for the first time in June 1945, was released by Him to humanity to enable us to invoke the energies which would change our world and make possible the return of the Christ and Hierarchy. This World Prayer, translated into many languages, is not sponsored by any group or sect. It is used daily by men and women of goodwill who wish to bring about right human relations among all humanity

FURTHER READING

The Reappearance of the Christ and the Masters of Wisdom
by Benjamin Creme
Creme's first book gives the background and pertinent information concerning the return of Maitreya, the Christ. A vast range of subjects is covered, including: the effect of the reappearance on the world's institutions, the antichrist and forces of evil, the soul and reincarnation, telepathy, nuclear energy, ancient civilizations, the problems of the developing world and a new economic order.
ISBN #0-936604-00-X, 256 pages

The Great Approach by Benjamin Creme
Describes the gradual transformation of our chaotic world under the influence of the Masters of Wisdom, who are returning openly to the world for the first time in 98,000 years. An extraordinary synthesis of knowledge, it throws a searchlight on the future and predicts our highest achievements of thought to reveal the amazing scientific discoveries which lie ahead. It shows us a world in which war is a thing of the past, and the needs of all are met.
ISBN #90-71484-23-8, 336 pages

Maitreya's Mission — Vol. I by Benjamin Creme
Presents further developments in the emergence of Maitreya and also covers a wide range of subjects, including the work and teachings of Maitreya, the externalization of the Masters, life ahead in the New Age, evolution and initiation, meditation and service, the Seven Rays.
ISBN #90-71484-08-4, 411 pages

Maitreya's Mission — Vol. II by Benjamin Creme
Offers unique information on such subjects as meditation, growth of consciousness, psychology, health, the environment, world service, and science and technology in the New Age. The process of Maitreya's public emergence is updated. Also explains such phenomena as crop circles, crosses of light, visions of the Madonna, healing wells, and UFOs. *ISBN #90-71484-11-4, 718 pages*

Maitreya's Mission — Vol. III by Benjamin Creme
A chronicle of the next millennium. Political, economic and social structures that will guarantee the necessities of life for all people. New ways of thinking that will reveal the mysteries of the universe and release our divine potential — all guided and inspired by Maitreya and the Masters of Wisdom. Includes a compilation of ray structures and

227

points of evolution of all 950 initiates given in *Maitreya's Mission*, Vols. I and II, and in *Share International* magazine.
ISBN #90-71484-15-7, 704 pages

Transmission: A Meditation for the New Age

by Benjamin Creme
Describes a dynamic group process of stepping down powerful spiritual energies directed by the Masters of Wisdom. Introduced by Benjamin Creme, at the request of his own Master, this potent world service stimulates both planetary transformation and personal growth of the individuals participating.
4th Edition. ISBN #90-71484-17-3, 204 pages

Messages from Maitreya the Christ

During the years of preparation for His emergence, Maitreya gave 140 Messages through Benjamin Creme during public lectures. The method used was mental overshadowing and the telepathic rapport thus set up. The Messages inspire readers to spread the news of His reappearance and to work urgently for the rescue of millions suffering from poverty and starvation in a world of plenty.
2nd Edition. ISBN #90-71484-22-X, 283 pages

A Master Speaks

Articles by Benjamin Creme's Master from the first 12 volumes of Share International magazine. The book includes such topics as: reason and intuition, health and healing, life in the New Age, glamour, human rights, Maitreya's mission, the role of man.
2nd Edition. ISBN #90-71484-10-6, 256 pages

The Ageless Wisdom Teaching by Benjamin Creme

This introduction to humanity's spiritual legacy covers the major principles: the Divine Plan, source of the teaching, evolution of human consciousness, the Spiritual Hierarchy, energies, the Seven Rays, karma, reincarnation, initiation, and more. Includes a glossary of esoteric terms. *ISBN #90-71484-13-0, 62 pages*

The above books have been translated and published in Arabic, Chinese, Dutch, French, German, Hebrew, Italian, Japanese, Romanian, Russian, Spanish, and Swedish by groups responding to this message. Further translations are in progress. Books, as well as audio and video cassettes, are available from local booksellers.

Share International

A UNIQUE MAGAZINE featuring each month: • up-to-date information about Maitreya, the World Teacher • an article from a Master of Wisdom • expansions of the esoteric teachings • articles by and interviews with people on the leading edge in every field of endeavour • news from UN agencies and reports of positive developments in the transformation of our world • Benjamin Creme's answers to a variety of topical questions submitted by subscribers and the public.

Share International brings together the two major directions of New Age thinking — the political and the spiritual. It shows the synthesis underlying the political, social, economic, and spiritual changes now occurring on a global scale, and seeks to stimulate practical action to rebuild our world along more just and compassionate lines.

Share International covers news, events, and comments bearing on Maitreya's priorities: an adequate supply of the right food, adequate housing and shelter for all, healthcare as a universal right, and the maintenance of ecological balance in the world.

Versions of *Share International* are available in Dutch, French, German, Japanese and Spanish. For subscription information, contact the appropriate office below. [ISSN #0169-1341]

Excerpts from the magazine are published on the World Wide Web at:
www.shareintl.org and *www.share-international.org*

For North, Central, and South America,
Australia, New Zealand and the Philippines
Share International
P.O. Box 971, North Hollywood CA 91603 USA

For the UK
Share International
P.O. Box 3677, London NW5 1RU UK

For the rest of the world
Share International
P.O. Box 41877, 1009 DB Amsterdam, Holland

INDEX

About the Author

Scottish-born painter and esotericist Benjamin Creme has for the last 27 years been preparing the world for the most extraordinary event in human history—the return of our spiritual mentors to the everyday world.

Creme has appeared on television, radio and in documentary films worldwide and lectures throughout Western and Eastern Europe, the USA, Japan, Australia, New Zealand, Canada and Mexico.

Trained and supervised over many years by his own Master, he began his public work in 1974. In 1982 he announced that the Lord Maitreya, the long-awaited World Teacher, was living in London, ready to present Himself openly when invited by the media to do so. This event is now imminent.

Benjamin Creme continues to carry out his task as messenger of this inspiring news. His books, ten at present, have been translated into many languages. He is also the editor of *Share International* magazine, which circulates in over 70 countries. He accepts no money for any of this work.

Benjamin Creme lives in London, is married, and has three children.